BLUEPRINTS ON FABRIC

innovative uses for cyanotype

BLUEPRINTS ON FABRIC

innovative uses for cyanotype

BARBARA HEWITT

 INTERWEAVE PRESS

Cover design, Signorella Graphic Arts
Photography, Joe Coca
Illustration, Susan Strawn
Design and production, Elizabeth R. Mrofka

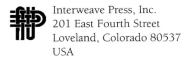 Interweave Press, Inc.
201 East Fourth Street
Loveland, Colorado 80537
USA

Printed in Hong Kong by Sing Cheong

Library of Congress Cataloging-in-Publication Data

Hewitt, Barbara.
      Blueprints on fabric / by Barbara Hewitt.
          p.   cm.
      Includes bibliographical references and index.
      ISBN 0-934026-91-2 : $12.95
      1. Textile printing.   I. Title.
   TT852.H48   1995
   746.6'2—dc20   94-48503
                                             CIP

First Printing: 10M:295:CC

ACKNOWLEDGEMENTS

John Basye, my husband and business partner, has been an inspiration and constant help in creating this book. Ronan Berri is my artistic soul mate and friend who has helped with printing and design ideas over the many years we have worked together. In addition, John and I wish to thank our collective family of seven children who have all helped in every aspect of our business.

CONTENTS

Introduction. 7
A Brief History of the Blueprint Process 12
Getting Ready. 17
Choosing and Preparing Design Sources. 29
Printing the Fabric 41
Fixing the Exposed Blueprint 58
Care of Blueprinted Fabric 68
Projects 72
Certificate of Chemical Safety. 94
Care Instructions 94
Bibliography. 95
Sources. 95
Index 96

INTRODUCTION

I became involved with blueprinting more than twenty years ago. To me, its appeal lay in the possibilities for interpreting fabric and fashion in exciting, dramatic, new ways. Up to that point, I had been working with fibers, stitchery, and knotting to make multi-level soft sculptures and wall hangings. I first showed my blueprints at a museum art fair. As I was preparing for the show, I wondered, "What am I going to wear?" I wanted to wear something distinctive. So, I decided to blueprint fabric for a long dress, using for the design large, overgrown onions I'd left in my garden over the winter. It gave a strikingly detailed image, even to the point of picking up the fine network of roots and bits of clinging dirt. Many people at that art show were more interested in what I was wearing than what I was exhibiting.

Printing T-shirts is a fun group activity. The shirt on the left was originally yellow, and the blueprint process resulted in a yellow design on a dark green background.

Continuing left to right, the shirts were originally white, fuchsia, turquoise, and light green.

A ruana is a versatile garment that can be worn as a shawl, a skirt, a dress, and perhaps some other ways I haven't thought of!

A transluscent silk window shade will keep glaring sun out of your eyes while letting some light through the window.

I immediately began experimenting with fabric design for clothing and haven't been able to stop since. The onions led to carrots which led to ferns which led to pine boughs and all sorts of weeds. I printed doilies and old lace, negatives of favorite family photos. I realized I was limited only by my imagination, and I can hardly walk down the street without looking for yet another type of grass or leaf. Printing possibilities are everywhere.

Some of my most challenging and rewarding projects have been commissions such as willow print seat covers for bent-willow garden furniture and commemorative pillows with appropriate photographs as appreciation gifts for a women's political fundraising event.

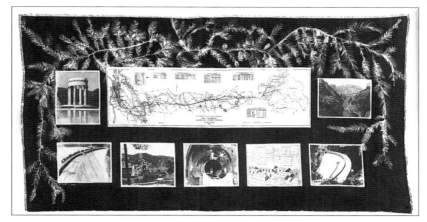

I printed this banner when there was talk of removing the O'Shaughnessy Dam in Yosemite National Park and dismantling the Hetch Hetchy water system that supplies San Francisco and much of the Peninsula.

I once designed curtains for a teenage girl's room. She had a very special room designed by her father. A puffy feather bed with an iron bedstead was tucked in an alcove next to an 8' high and 10' wide wood-framed arched window overlooking a secluded garden. Using a cotton lace curtain, butterfly drawings, birch leaves, and confetti stars, I printed the panels to look as if blowing lace curtains framed a window open to the night sky. It gave her privacy while maintaining the illusion of open space. It was a fantasy window within a window.

I've even used blueprinting to make political statements. Slogans, photographs, maps, etc. can be printed on fabric banners for rallies and exhibits.

Celebrate your family history by printing a memory quilt.

The cyanotype photographic process is a dynamic art form. Teachers, painters, photographers, craftspeople, and artists can utilize blueprinting techniques in innovative ways.

The comfort and sentiment of old family quilts inspires modern quilters. With blueprinting, they can celebrate their family history by creating memory quilts. A blue or brown-toned photo-print on soft cotton has a nostalgic look reminiscent of the original ancestral photographs.

Quiltmaking is popular in many school and community projects. Members can contribute their blueprinted squares to be quilted and used as a commemorative display or to raffle for fundraising. Blueprinting also has great potential for school study projects. Teachers can use the process to reinforce science, nature, and history lessons.

Blueprinting presents great opportunity for amusing visuals. Ansel looks quite pleased on his seafood tablecloth.

Genealogists might want to create a visual family tree. A photographic set-up of ancestors and their descendants accompanied by pertinent dates can be arranged on glass. Then a series of copies can be printed for family members.

A recent calligraphers convention was saluted with blueprinted circle T-shirts. Garden club members can blueprint their favorite foliage on shirts or aprons.

Try blueprinting. It is fun, easy, instantly rewarding, not too expensive, and a great way to step into a new realm of creativity. I believe that most of us have strong creative urges. Sometimes these urges lie dormant because we hesitate to express ourselves. Cyanotype allows the creative process to move forward whether or not you can draw or have a sophisticated education in art or photography. I believe it is important to leave a legacy of self expression, especially in the gifts we present to others. Too much in our world is mass produced. Let blueprinting be a lasting imprint of you!

Sunflowers straight from the garden enliven this playful jumper.

A BRIEF HISTORY OF THE BLUEPRINT PROCESS

The dark blue impression known as blueprint or cyanotype, which many of us think of in relation to the architectural field, is one of the most permanent photographic processes known. The cyanotype is a wonderfully simple process that uses ferric ammonium citrate and potassium ferricyanide. The chemicals are applied to a surface and dried. An object or negative is placed on top of the treated surface and the composition is exposed to the sun. Then simply rinsing the exposed article with water fixes the image and makes it permanent. The process was invented in 1842 by English astronomer Sir John Herschel.

In 1839, Herschel received a letter from his friend William Henry Fox Talbot, informing him of his discovery of an innovative photogenic drawing process and predicting its widespread use as an inexpensive alternative to the printing press.

Talbot's process, "calotype", involved the use of potassium iodine, silver nitrate, glacial-acetic acid, and water. While the ability to accurately reproduce images on paper was a remarkable breakthrough, the process was somewhat complicated and produced inconsistent results.

At about the same time Talbot was developing his process, French artist Louis Jacques Mandé Daguerre announced his discovery of a method of capturing images on silver-plated copper. While the "daguerreotype" produced a more true-to-the-original image than did Talbot's photogenic drawing, it was not useful for the production of books or other matter printed on paper— the images appeared on metal plates and could not be readily reproduced.

Herschel embraced these new developments as the answer to his search for a method other than hand-copying to make

Carix [America] ca. 1850   Gleichenia flabellata [Australia] ca. 1850

Photographs of two of Anna Atkins' blueprints. Courtesy Fraenkel Gallery, San Franciso, CA.

copies of his intricate calculations and other memoranda. He furthered the study and contributed to it with his invention of the cyanotype, which he called "positive photographic tracings" and used the method in much the same way as we use copying machines today.

Herschel's work with cyanotype came to the attention of John George Children, a highly respected scientist and a Fellow and Secretary of the Royal Society whose purpose was to establish standards for scientific inquiry. Accounts of advances in blueprinting technology were published as they happened, and Children, with his long-standing interest in chemistry, was quick to learn about the mechanics and potential of photography. He passed this knowledge on to his daughter, Anna Children Atkins.

Anna Atkins began her work with cyanotype for the documentation of British plants. "Botany, and particularly the study of algae, was at least one area of scientific endeavor where women were cautiously welcomed." In her introduction to the resulting book, *Photographs of British Algae: Cyanotype Impressions,* she says that "the difficulty of making accurate drawings of objects as minute as many of the Algae and Conferva, has induced me to avail myself of Sir John Herschel's beautiful process of Cyanotype, to obtain impressions of the plants themselves, which I have much pleasure in offering to my botanical friends." *Photographs of British Algae* was the first book ever produced by photocopy methods, and the use of this photographic process allowed Atkins to present the outline of the plants with absolute accuracy. She produced the prints, and it was up to each individual to organize the plates and bind them together.

While she began her project for the

sharing of botanical information, Atkins' imagination and flair make even these scientific prints works of art. In later work, Anna printed not only plants, but feathers and lace as well.

Many of the prints from the original collection are still in excellent condition and were reproduced in the 1985 book, *Sun Gardens,* by Larry J. Schaaf.

The first commercial blueprint machine was introduced to the United States by a Swiss firm at the Philadelphia Centennial Exposition in 1876. Blueprinting as a part of industry had a very slow start; the prints were at first viewed as a curiosity rather than a viable means of reproduction.

When the industrial revolution was in full swing, blueprints came into general use by architects, builders, and engineers. Up to that point, it was thought that the sun was the only means of exposure, and cloudy or rainy days could seriously delay projects. Need prompted invention and in 1903 engineers came up with the idea of using the Cooper-Hewitt mercury vapor lamp for exposing blueprints.

Blueprint machines at the turn of the century were magnificent mechanical monsters as were most machines of the era. (Have you ever seen a pencil sharpener from the 1880s?) The blueprint machines were vertically oriented and had glass suspended in heavy sliding frames for loading and unloading originals. Later, a machine was developed using a felt-covered cylinder with a roll of tracing cloth to hold the blueprint paper and original in tight contact as they were passed by a bank of carbon arc lamps. A celluloid carrier was used in another machine for a short time until it burned up in a puff of smoke.

About 1910, three new machines were

introduced to the market. These machines combined printing, washing, potashing, rinsing, and drying. The machines needed gas, electricity, and water. The evenness of light, heat of dryer drums, flow of water, and time of exposure were all manually juggled; blueprint operators had to be alert, nimble, and quick.

Although blueprinting was a fast, easy method of reproduction that cost only pennies per square foot, the dark blue background posed some problems. It was difficult to make legible notes and corrections, and prints of renderings could not be colored for presentation. Special paper negatives were developed that could produce white background copies, and the process continued to be used until the early 1960s to produce quick, useful reproductions.

Blueprints used by architects and engineers today are actually diazo prints or ozalids and are "whiteprints", not blue. Diazo was created in Germany in the 1930s. It is a process related to blueprinting—it produces a direct positive print. The paper has a faster reaction to light than blueprint paper, and the process uses aniline dyes developed in ammonia fumes. The whole process is more streamlined than blueprinting, and there are continual improvements in coatings and films. The main drawback of diazo prints is that they are not archival—the print is not permanent. The cyanotype (blueprint) process presented in this book uses the original, historic formula. The print is permanent.

GETTING READY

The chemicals used in blueprinting are safe and readily available from chemical supply houses. The equipment consists of common household items.

THE CHEMISTRY OF BLUEPRINTING

Blueprinting is a surprisingly simple two-step chemical process. A water-based solution of green ferric ammonium citrate and potassium ferricyanide is applied to paper or natural fiber cloth and allowed to dry. When exposed to ultraviolet light, the ferric iron of the citrate is reduced to the ferrous state. After exposure, the exposed paper or cloth is rinsed in water, and an insoluble iron salt, ferroferricyanide, is formed which permanently stains the surface. The color of this new iron salt is called Prussian Blue.

The real fun begins when you place an opaque or semi-opaque object on top of the pretreated fabric and then expose it to the sun. The object blocks the light, preventing the first chemical change, and the following water rinse clears the chemical out. The result is a high-resolution "copy" of the object. Think of the possibilities!

These chemicals are easy and safe to use and are readily available from chemical supply houses. Ferric ammonium citrate is most often used as an iron and vitamin supplement and is no more than a minor irritant to humans because it is sticky. Potassium ferriccyanide is a stable compound that only presents a health hazard if it is heated above 300°C (572°F)—domestic ovens do not exceed 500°F—or if it is combined with an acid to form toxic hydrogen cyanide. Because the blueprinting process calls for neither heating the chemicals nor combining

with acid, you can feel comfortable dealing with the solution and treated fabric. Some published formulas for the blueprint process suggest using potassium dicromate as a color enhancer. This is a toxic substance unnecessary to the process and I do not recommend its use.

If this still sounds too scientific and scary, take heart; you can simply buy the fabric pretreated! (See "Sources" on page 95.) If you do purchase and prepare your own chemical formulas, read the Materials and Safety Data Sheet guidelines that accompany each chemical order.

CHOOSING PRINTABLE SURFACES

Blueprinting only works on natural fibers such as cotton, silk, linen, and viscose/rayon. You can print on yardage, ready-made clothes, household linens, tote bags—

Choose natural fibers. Shown here from top to bottom, are white cotton, turquoise cotton, natural raw silk, and fuchsia cotton. From left to right, the fabrics are untreated, treated but not printed, printed but not rinsed, and finished.

the possibilities are endless.

Synthetic fibers will not print. Cotton/polyester blends will print, but the blue will not be as intense as with 100% natural fibers. This is because polyester fiber does not react with the blueprint chemical; therefore, only the cotton part of the fabric will print. Blueprinted cotton/polyester-blend fabrics will "fade" more readily because the cotton component tends to erode during wear and washing, exposing the unprinted polyester.

Canvas will print, but because the fibers are tightly woven and repel water, it is difficult to completely saturate canvas with the blueprint solution and it is equally difficult to rinse completely after the print has been made.

Whatever fabric you choose to use, make sure it is clean and free of any sizing or conditioners. Wash and rinse the fabric in hot water with a small amount of liquid, non-phosphate, non-sodium soap. Be sure to wash all

Note the difference in the intensity of blue between the 100% cotton T-shirt on the left and the 50% cotton/50% polyester sweatshirt.

starch and sizing finishes out of new T-shirts and clothes. If you don't remove all the sizing, the blueprint chemical will not be absorbed evenly, leaving blotchy, brownish-yellow tones on the finished print. It is always best to test small samples of whatever fiber you choose before undertaking a large project. Take notes about procedures in order to reproduce results.

P R E P A R I N G   A   W O R K   A R E A

Many things can be stained with blueprint chemicals. You may print your floor, walls, counters, clothes, and shoes—intentionally or not. Cover counters and floors with newspapers or drop cloths, cover yourself with work clothes, rubber gloves, and a particle dust mask. Then have fun!

Here's a list of the equipment you should have handy:

- Glass or plastic bowls
- Glass or plastic measuring cups
- Plastic spoon for stirring (Wooden spoons absorb liquid blueprint solution, turn blue, and are impossible to clean.)
- Scale (accurate kitchen or postal)
- Synthetic paint brush (The solution will stain natural bristle brushes. When your brush is blue, it is hard to see if it is clean.)
- Sponge (new)
- Black-and-white newspapers or plain, absorbent paper
- A household laundry dryer or light-proof room or closet equipped with a clothesline
- Plastic clothesline and pins
- Rubber gloves
- Particle dust mask

First add the potassium ferricyanide to warm water and stir until totally dissolved.

Gradually add the ferric ammonium citrate by sprinkling a small amount on the surface, stirring it until it dissolves, adding a bit more, and stirring again.

Choose a clean work space away from direct sunlight. Although the blueprint chemicals will react in florescent and incandescent light, the reaction is slow, so you can make preparations with the lights on. Use clean and dry measuring, mixing, and storage containers of glass or plastic that are reserved for blueprinting only. Do not use metal containers as iron salts in the solution may react with the metal—especially aluminum—and taint the solution.

PREPARING THE BLUEPRINT SOLUTION

Before you begin, put on rubber gloves and a particle dust mask to protect yourself from inhaling airborne chemical dust. To blueprint a small piece of fabric (about a yard, depending on width and weight), pour eight ounces of warm water into a container. Measure and add one-half ounce of potassium ferricyanide. Stir until dissolved. Measure out one ounce of green ferric ammonium citrate. Gradually add the ferric ammonium citrate by sprinkling a small amount on the surface, stirring it until it dissolves, adding a bit more, and stirring again.

One gallon of solution will treat approximately 12 yards of fabric. This estimate is based on processing 54"-wide, medium-weight cotton sheeting and squeezing out the excess liquid using an electric wringer. If you want to mix the solution in large quantity, use the following formulas:

White five-gallon buckets (the type used for house paint) are good for mixing large volumes. Against a white background, it's easy to see whether or not the chemicals are dissolved. Larger amounts are difficult to lift and pour without spills. But be aware that white plastic buckets are not light-proof. Either cover the bucket with thick, black, opaque plastic, or transfer the contents to a light-proof container. *Be sure to stir the solution well before each use.*

Water	Potassium Ferricyanide	Ferric Ammonium Citrate
1/2 gal.	4 oz.	8 oz.
(2 qts.)	(1/4 lb.)	(1/2 lb.)
4^1/$_2$ gal.	2 lbs.	4 lbs.
6^1/$_2$ gal.	3 lbs.	6 lbs.
8^1/$_2$ gal.	4 lbs.	8 lbs.
10^1/$_2$ gal.	5 lbs.	10 lbs.
15 gal.	7^1/$_2$ lbs.	15 lbs.

After you've mixed the solution, clean up the work area and put away all of the chemicals to prevent light exposure, dampness, or spills.

After the chemicals have been mixed and the original containers closed, it is safe to remove your dust mask. But you should keep your gloves on until after the fabric has been treated and dried to avoid staining your hands.

Applying the Blueprint Solution to Your Fabric

Once the chemicals are mixed, you are ready to apply the solution to the fabric. Because the solution is light-reactive, try to work with only the amount you need for the current project. Keep excess solution stored in a light-proof container. Add more solution only as needed. *Stir replacement chemicals before adding them to an existing solution, then stir both to evenly blend.* Because the salts separate when left standing, stirring is essential to keep the formula balanced.

There are several ways to apply the solution to the fabric. The goal here is to cover the fabric evenly and thoroughly. All of the methods described below give good results, the difference being the ease with which they work for different amounts of fabric being treated.

Submersion

This methods works best for small pieces—a few quilt squares, a T-shirt, or a pillow cover or case—and is by far the simplest application method.

Stir the blueprint solution and pour enough in a plastic or glass container to cover the fabric. Be sure to use a container large enough to hold your project. Submerge the fabric in the solution and use your gloved hands to move it around several minutes until it is thoroughly saturated. Large pieces of fabric tend to fold and crumple, blocking the solution's ability to saturate and result in a "tie-dyed" effect—this can be an interesting look, but only if it's one you want.

Once the fabric is saturated, use your

Dip a clean, dry, synthetic brush into the blueprint solution, then press it against the side of the container to remove excess liquid.

Brush chemicals on with long, even strokes. Apply the solution as evenly as possible and be sure to completely saturate the fabric.

hands to squeeze out as much liquid as possible and then smooth it out to remove creases.

PAINTING

Use this method for large projects, say, fabric-by-the-yard, or if you don't have a container large enough for submersion.

Stir the blueprint chemicals well. In a plastic or glass bowl, pour enough solution to cover the surface to be painted (about one cup per yard). Remember not to pour out more chemical than needed, and keep unused supplies covered and out of the light.

If more chemical solution is needed during painting, *stir first* and then add the new supply to the bowl and *stir again*. The solution that is in the bowl will have had some light exposure and be a darker green than that in the supply container. However, if you thoroughly mix the new solution with the old and work quickly, this is not a problem.

Dip a clean, dry, synthetic brush into the blueprint solution, then press it against the side of the bowl to remove excess liquid. By removing excess liquid from the brush and holding it at an angle as you work, it will not release all of the liquid at once in a puddle. Brush chemicals on with long, even strokes. Apply the solution as evenly as possible and be sure to completely saturate the fabric.

An interesting effect results from saturating only part of the surface and letting the brush strokes show along the edges. However, these edges may turn slightly brown during exposure, especially in hot weather, because the solution is thinner than elsewhere.

S P O N G I N G

If you don't have a paint brush, you can apply the solution with a sponge. As with painting, this method will work well with both large and small projects. Pour out a suitable amount of solution as for painting, above. Using a *new, dry* sponge, dip the sponge into the blueprint solution and press it against the side of the bowl or wring it to remove excess liquid. A dripping wet sponge will make puddles of solution and will result in an uneven application. Wipe long, smooth strokes across the fabric to get an even application.

W R I N G I N G

In my studio, I remove excess blueprint solution by running the fabric through the wringer of an old-fashioned washer. Wringers are good for applying the solution thoroughly and evenly to both large and small pieces of fabric. Simply dip the fabric into the solution and then fold the fabric so that it is pulled through the wringer evenly. After the first pass, refold the fabric in a different direction and put it through the wringer again to distribute the solution evenly. A large piece of fabric may require several passes.

The wringer rollers should be cleaned before and after each session, even if the wringer is used only for blueprint fabric processing. Wringer pads will absorb the chemicals and affect pieces that come in contact with them later. Run a wet, clean rag or towel through the wringer and wipe off the surface around it.

Once your fabric has been treated, you can print it right away (see "Blueprinting Wet Fabric" page 54), dry it before printing, or dry the fabric and store it for later use. If you want to reserve the treated fabric for future use, you must store it in a light-proof container. Photography film and paper is packaged in black, light-proof bags that are ideal for fabric storage. Check with your local photographic lab—some will give away their supply of empty bags.

DRYING TREATED FABRIC

Make a dark room away from sunlight for drying. Any areas of the treated fabric

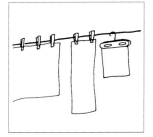

Hang the blueprint-treated fabric on a plastic clothesline with plastic clothespins or use a pant hanger.

that are exposed to light will begin to change color immediately.

Cover the floor to collect drips, and allow the fabric to hang straight without being folded or touching anything. Hang the fabric on a plastic clothesline with plastic clothespins or use a pant hanger. Cotton line and wooden clothes pins will absorb the blueprint solution from the fabric and you will not be able to reuse them.

Small pieces of treated fabric can be dried with a hair dryer. Yardage can be dried in a household clothes dryer. Set the dryer on the coolest heat setting possible and dry three yards of cotton for approximately thirty minutes, three yards of silk for about fifteen minutes. After the treated fabric is dry, wash and dry the machine drum, back wall, and door. If you don't clean the dryer, your next load of laundry will have blue stains.

STORING MIXED CHEMICALS

Once you've treated all the fabric planned for your session, you must properly store the leftover solution. The chemicals are shipped in brown, glass containers. When empty, these containers can be used to store the excess mixed solution. Heavy, dark plastic kitchenware pitchers with lids can also be used. Put a secondary, light-proof cover over the lid to ensure that no light enters. A good choice for this secondary cover is black UV-opaque plastic, 4 millimeters thick, sold as visqueen at building supply stores. To test for lightfastness, hold it up and look through it straight at the sun. If any light is visible, even a faint circle, it is not light-proof. Double the plastic and look again.

Keep separate mixing and storing containers for your blueprint solutions—do not return them to kitchen use. Store mixed chemicals in a dark place. Label and date the containers and keep them out of reach of children and pets who might accidently spill them. Unused blueprint solution can be stored for three to six months in a cool or cold (not freezing) location.

Before using stored solution, *stir it well* and test it on a small fabric scrap before undertaking a project. If the solution has turned dark green while in storage, it will still print, but the area exposed to light may be dull blue and the unexposed, normally white area may be stained a medium blue. If there is lint in the solution, strain it through a filter—a coffee filter or cheese cloth in a strainer or sieve will do the trick—to avoid getting lint spots on your next project. (Dried, treated fabric may be stored up to five years and still print, but the sooner it is used, the brighter the print will be. The best results will be obtained if the fabric is used within three to six months.)

Dispose of solution that contains mold or that has been exposed to light for thirty minutes or more. The unused blueprint so-lution should be rinsed down a drain with copious amounts of water. Dilute with at least eight times more water than solution. *Do not pour the solution into the ground or down a storm drain.* If there is more than one cup of blueprint chemical solution to dis-pose of, do it at the rate of one cup per day. Most treatment plants are limited by feder-al regulations to the amount of cyanide com-pounds that they can release in a given pe-riod. The same rules apply to disposal into septic tanks.

The fish print at top was made with freshly treated fabric, and the portraits below with treated fabric that had been dried and stored for six years.

CHOOSING AND PREPARING DESIGN SOURCES

NATURE PRINTS

Nature prints are intriguing and timeless. There is enormous variety in the plant life around us. If you take the time to look closely, you'll be delighted with the intricate structures of leaves and flowers, with their balance and grace.

Over the many years I've spent designing clothes with nature prints, I've found that people are most attracted to simple prints that convey the qualities and memories of a favorite tree or flower. Bold or delicate, we respond to prints that complement our appearances and personalities. Blueprinting allows us to capture the natural beauty and movement of plant life, a part of life that we depend upon physically, emotionally, and visually.

So, let's explore how to get some really good nature prints. The first objective is to find a subject with an interesting shape. It

Most types of leaves make interesting blueprint designs.

may be a leaf: maple, ivy, sycamore, ginkgo. It may be clusters of leaves: California pepper, nandina, schefflera; or even branches with leaves: eucalyptus, birch, Chinese elm. Palm fronds that sweep across nine or ten feet of space in strong, bold strokes are good candidates as are evergreens: cedar, juniper, and pine. Each has distinct characteristics. Ferns are wonderful choices but temperamental; they print best when pressed and dried. I also love to use weeds, native grasses, and all kinds of miniature plants that I find growing uncultivated by the roadside. Explore and you may find, as I have, many treasures—marsh grasses ten inches high near San Francisco Bay's pro-

A cluster of dried leaves make a dramatic design on a raw silk blouse.

tected recesses, and ten feet high or more on the Mendocino coast where they are toughened by the Pacific coast sea and wind.

In searching for nature objects, I consider the project and the scale that would be suitable. Is an all-over print called for? An accent to accompany a photo? A repetition for a border? Am I making a throw pillow for a cabin? A quilt? A shirt for a friend? I collect some foliage, bring it inside, and arrange it on a plain shirt or a pillow, or hold it up against the wall to evaluate my composition. An arrangement that looks perfectly acceptable outdoors is sometimes overwhelming when brought inside.

Most plants produce great quantities of leaves that should be pruned if the blueprint is to be successful. Overlapping layers of leaves or dense masses of evergreen needles will not reveal a plant's characteristic shapes. For a print to be effective, you must be selective. Light must be able to penetrate around stems and leaves (or needles) to reveal the remaining distinctive patterns. You may have to thin stems and leaves (or needles) so that the remaining shapes are clearly printed.

Because nature prints are botanical profiles, branches and leaves look best when positioned as they appear in nature. Even so, you will want to play around with your arrangement and use your selective eye to produce a pleasing composition.

FABRICS

Scores of fabrics exhibit interesting effects with the blueprinting process. Consider lace, doilies, fishnet, loosely woven fabrics, and cut-out scraps of fabric. Any fabric that allows some light to penetrate will produce a print.

One of my favorite projects is to print a

garment using an already-blueprinted fabric for the design source to create a reverse image on the next print. This technique is most effective when the design source is a blueprint on white fabric. Sunlight will pass through the white areas of the print and be mostly blocked by the blue area. The result is a reverse of the original blueprint.

The print-on-a-print will also capture the

Any fabric that allows some light to penetrate can be used as a design source.

Positive and negative images are created by printing with an already blueprinted fabric. The tank dress on the right was then brown-toned (see pages 65-67).

An assortment of colors and textures can be achieved by using colored fabric, textured fabric as a design element, and varying exposure times.

weave structure of the original cloth. Therefore, select interesting, natural fiber for your initial print. Cheesecloth, gauze, and lace are all good candidates. The result will be a collage of multiple textures and images.

In the tank dress shown at top left, I used clusters of leaves on an alternating open- and closed-weave cotton fabric to create the initial print. Next, I treated a white rayon tank dress with blueprint solution and let it dry. The printed cotton was placed over two-thirds of the dress front, smoothed down snugly against the dress surface, and pinned around the edges. Fresh leaves were pinned in place on top of the printed fabric as well as on the third of the dress not covered by the cloth. The resulting print has both positive and negative images.

Another interesting design source is a piece of fabric from which holes have been cut. The "holey" fabric can be placed on top

of another design set-up, and two minutes before exposure time is complete, removed to allow the sun to expose the area that had been covered. The resulting print will appear to have a subtle circular background texture.

FOUND OBJECTS

Any object that blocks light will form a print, and many objects have visually stimulating silhouettes. When ideas and visuals come together, the format for blueprints begins.

Children will enjoy using school supplies, mix-and-match plastic forms, dolls, toy box contents, and "junk drawer" treasures. Teens may want to use models, tool box supplies, work bench contents, kitchen utensils, and sewing box supplies. Cooks may favor the contents of pasta shelves at the market, and gardeners will want to explore nettings and

Almost any flat object can be used as a design source—plastic toys, fans, feathers, nets, cookie cutters, stencils, etc. Let your imagination soar.

This apron was designed with the pasta cook in mind.

garden tools as well as plants.

Also consider ground pepper, crystals, cut crystal bowls (best printed with the sun directly overhead), paper cut-outs, wrought-iron fences, antique jewelry, ribbons, fans, cookie cutters, fluorescent light reflective covers, eye glasses, furnace filters, chicken wire, expanded metal lath, unbuttered pop corn, paper clips. Beware of silk and plastic flowers—though readily available and appealing, their structure can be so regular that the prints look fake.

Garden netting produces an interesting grid background pattern that can be combined with other design sources. Extra care needs to be taken to pin the netting for tight contact with the fabric. I have made many, many jumpers with plastic netting topped by puzzle pieces, popcorn, alphabet and wagon wheel pasta. I have also made jumpers with starry night themes (confetti stars, a new moon cut-out, and a border of dried flower "trees") and workshop themes (borders with hammers, wrenches, screwdrivers, and other interesting tools).

Don't let the bright color of an object prevent you from observing its shape. You can see the shape that an object will print by looking at its shadow. Avoid bulky items that can't be pinned or propped up perpendicular to the sun. Distinct prints are made only if the objects are well-pinned directly to the fabric and oriented perpendicular to the sun.

FILM, DRAWINGS, AND TEXT

I love using film. Photos, drawings, and text can be reproduced on film for a huge variety of design options.

FILM

In choosing photographs for design sources, choose ones with clear, well-focused images—the final blueprint can never be sharper than the original. Photographs can be old or new, black-and-white or color. You can edit or crop a photograph, enlarge or reduce it. Slides can be converted to prints using a color laser copier at a copy shop. You can make a positive print,

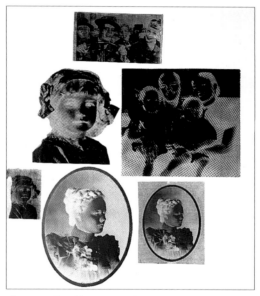

Photographic film is ideal for blueprinting. You can edit or crop a photograph, enlarge or reduce it. You can make a positive print—one that looks like the original photograph—from a film negative. Positive film (shown at top) will produce a negative print; one which reverses the light and dark values of the original photograph.

which looks like the original, or a negative print, which reverses the light and dark values of the original. Although some of the terminology used in this section may cause confusion, especially because some words are used interchangeably, I have tried to make this as user-friendly as possible.

MAKING NEGATIVE FILM FOR POSITIVE PRINTS

If you want a positive print, one that looks like the original photograph (except that it is blue and white), you will first have to make a film negative. (Even if the original photograph is in color, you will need a black-and-white negative. Color film contains red, yellow, blue, and black tones that will not produce recognizable images through the blueprint process.) An inexpensive approach is to have a halftone negative made of the photograph. A halftone is made by photographing the image through a glass plate containing a grid of very fine lines that breaks the subject into thousands of tiny

black squares. In general, the finer the grid, or screen, the better the detail. However, fabric has a much rougher surface than photographic papers, and the blueprinting exposure time is quite long compared to

A piece of lace fabric and a film negative give old-fashioned charm to a blueprinted silk shawl.

darkroom work. Therefore, the best blue-prints are produced with 65-, 85-, or at most 100-line halftone screens.

Halftone negatives can be made by most full-service photocopy stores, photostat services, or lithographers. If you have several pictures of similar size and quality (for example, a collection of old family photographs), you can save money by grouping them together on one large piece of film. Later, you can cut them apart and print them individually.

Standard black-and-white film is called "continuous line" and ranges from clear to black. It distinguishes hundreds of shades of gray which in turn blueprint hundreds of shades of blue. If the original photograph is of good quality, continuous line film will blueprint well. You can get this kind of negative made at a photography lab.

Photographers and screen printers are familiar with Kodalith film. This film is pure black and transparent—there are no grey tones. A blueprint made from this type of film will be white where the film is black and blue where the film is clear. It will produce no intermediate shades. As with black-and-white negatives, Kodalith negatives can be made at photography labs.

You can also produce negatives on some color laser copiers. Be aware that there are several manufacturers of color laser copiers and that they all have different capabilities. It is important that you ask for a black-and-white negative transparency. A Xerox Color Laser Copier #5775 can be programmed to "Creative Mode, Negative Image" to produce the necessary negative.

Negative film can also be produced by computer imaging. Hardware and software are available that scan photographs and reproduce the images in negative form, which then can be printed onto a transparency sheet.

Our high-tech world also offers digital imaging which can produce some very fine results. Although the costs are presently quite high, this technique offers the greatest opportunity to recover faded, obscure prints. Check your phone book, computer networking magazines, and graphic designers for available sources.

MAKING POSITIVE FILM FOR NEGATIVE PRINTS

If you want to reverse the light and dark images and make a negative print, you will have to first make a film positive of your original image. This can be done on a regular copy machine. Simply copy your photograph onto transparent film. If you have a laser printer, you can also print images from your computer onto transparent film. (See glossary, page 49.)

Copy machines and laser printers work by depositing a layer of toner on the surface of the transparency (or paper). But the density and adhesive qualities of the toner vary with each machine. The best blueprints are made from dense prints. To determine if a transparency is dense enough for blueprinting, hold the printed transparency up to the light. You should not be able to see through the black areas. If you can, imme-

Most any drawing can be used as a design element. But remember that the blueprinted image made with positive film will reverse the light and dark tones of a drawing.

diately make a second transparency without moving or changing the original copy or machine settings. You will have two identical prints which you can then bond together with spray mount or cellophane tape to double the black density.

DRAWINGS AND TEXT

You can blueprint drawings and text following the same principles that apply for blueprinting photos. Keep in mind that if you want the text or drawing to print as positive—blue letters or lines on a white field—your film will have to be a negative image. Acetate is easy to work with and can be drawn directly onto with opaque markers, rubylith ink, or grease pencils.

You need to be aware that the edge of the film or transparency will show as a thin line in a blueprint. If this is not a desired effect, simply cut the image out or produce it on a piece of film that is larger than the area of fabric to be printed so that the edges of the film are outside the print area.

While film and transparencies are easy to work with, you cannot use them on wet fabric. The moisture in wet, blueprint-treated fabric must evaporate during exposure in the sun. Because film is nonporous, it will inhibit drying, and what moisture does evaporate will condense under the film and

Try combining different types of design sources. Positive film made from drawings, confetti stars, and plant material were used to make this dinosaur T-shirt.

spoil the image. To make matters worse, this moisture can dissolve the toner and destroy the image on copy-machine or laser-printer produced transparencies.

Cellulose acetate films are insoluble in water and expand in heat. It is therefore im-portant to secure the film in tight contact with the fabric while printing. If the film lifts off the fabric during exposure, the image will be blurred. (See "Film" on page 44.)

GLOSSARY

Acetate Transparency–clear, transparency film that can be purchased in office, graphic art, and art supply stores. It is available by the sheet or by the box. Check the manufacturer and model to determine correct weight film. The wrong weight can melt in a copier. Copy shops stock their own supply.

Acetate–a salt or ester of acetic acid. Cellulose acetate is used for making textile fibers, packaging sheets, photographic films, and varnishes.

Cellophane Tape–a transparent tape that will not show in blueprints. Look for the words "cellophane" or "transpar-ent" on labels. Other types of tape will show in the print.

Cellulose–a polysaccharide of glucose that constitutes the chief part of the cell walls of plants. It occurs naturally in such fibrous substances as cotton and kapok, and is the raw material of many manufactured goods (paper, rayon, and cellophane).

Film–cellulose acetate or cellulose nitrate which has been coated with radiation- (ultraviolet) sensitive emulsion for taking photographs.

Print–the finished photograph made from exposed and developed film.

PRINTING THE FABRIC

PREPARING A SUPPORT BASE FOR PRINTING

Your treated fabric will need to be secured onto a support base to keep it flat and stable during the printing process. The base should be sturdy and nonflexible, have a porous, flat surface, be sized proportionate to the project, and be of manageable weight. You will pin the fabric to this base, arrange the design on top of it, and move the whole works to the light source.

Fiberglass insulation board (available at building supply centers) makes a good, lightweight support base. It comes in 4-by-8-foot sheets of different thicknesses—a thickness of $1^1/2''$ is adequate to hold most pins and stable enough to be propped up without additional support. Extensions can be attached to the original board by inserting dowels for stability, gluing the sections together, and then taping over the seams.

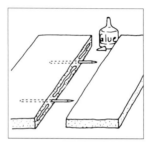

Attach an extension to a fibergalss insulation board support base by inserting dowels through the sections, glueing the sections together, and then taping over the seams with duct tape.

Wrap the support board with two layers of black-and-white newprint or plain craft paper, and secure the paper in place with pins or cellophane tape.

Insulation board can be reused many times and can be easily cut with a sharp knife to the size you need. Insulation board is usually covered with aluminum foil that has writing on it. Before you begin, wrap the board with black-and-white newsprint or plain craft paper to cover the writing on the foil. Otherwise, the foil will reflect light that penetrates through the weave of the fabric onto the back of the cloth, leaving a reverse image of the writing on the fabric.

If you are printing wet fabric (see pages 54-56), the newsprint or craft paper will also absorb excess moisture. This is an important advantage because if the foil gets wet, puddles of liquid will form under the fabric and distort the printed image. If the paper becomes damp and wrinkled, turn it over or replace it with dry paper before printing the next project—deep ridges in wrinkled paper and chemical deposits will make the blueprint color uneven.

Styrofoam also makes a good support base. It has the same properties as insulation board, but tends to break apart with repeated use. Styrofoam can be purchased in sheets of different sizes from hobby supply shops or building supply centers. Thin slabs

of styrofoam can be mounted on top of sheets of corrugated packaging material for added depth and rigidity. Use smooth, flat pieces just slightly larger than the fabric you're printing.

Corrugated boxes or sheets work well as support bases as long as they are clean, flat, and dry. But I've found them to have two serious drawbacks. Some corrugated boxes, particularly those used for packaging heavy objects, are reinforced with glue. The glue makes them so rigid that you may have trouble getting pins to penetrate the surface. Additionally, large corrugated pieces are easily bent or creased which prevents the fabric from laying flat. However, this usually isn't a problem with small projects.

Cover whatever base you choose with two layers of newspaper or one layer of craft paper and secure the paper with pins or tape so that it won't blow around during exposure. Place the fabric you intend to blue-print on the paper-covered base, stretch it taut, and pin the edges securely with T-pins.

NOTES ON PINNING BOARDS AND FILM

I have found that after repeated use pinning boards begin to crumble and sag, even if wrapped in paper for protection. This is not a problem for nature and found-object prints, but film prints require that the support base be smooth to allow a tight contact that will prevent blurred images. When I print T- and sweat shirts, I put a felt pad (1/4"-thick foam rubber would also be effective) on top of the board first to smooth out any irregularities, then put the shirt on top of that, then the film, and finally the glass.

SET-UP

Set up the designs on the treated fabric indoors, away from direct sunlight. Plan the designs ahead of time so that the fabric is exposed to light as little as possible—try to complete the design set-up within fifteen to thirty minutes.

The most important goal in design set-up is to secure all design elements in a way that will keep them from falling off while they are moved to the light source or blown by the wind during outdoor exposure.

NATURE PRINTS

For nature prints, have a selection of pins available: T-pins (1" and $1^1/_2$" long) to hold branches in place, and pearl-headed sewing pins to anchor delicate stems and leaves. Position pins next to and slightly across branches, stems, and leaves so that they won't show in the finished print. Use pearl-headed pins next to the lighter weight stems and push them into the support so that they hold the plant tightly to the fabric surface. Pin branches and stems every three or four inches to ensure a flowing, continuous line image. Leaves can be anchored by positioning the pin heads over the leaves so that they will not show in the print. Leave 1/8" of space between the leaf and the fabric to avoid getting brown stains on the fabric from the pins. If there is no wind, you can choose not to pin leaves, allowing the sunlight to enter around their edges, creating beautiful, three-dimensional effects.

Freshly cut stems sometimes ooze moisture or sap, causing a stain on the fabric. Sap can be removed with acetone or nail polish remover, but the stain remains.

Do not cover fresh leaves with glass. The result will be a flat image without shadows and condensed moisture from the leaves can spoil the print.

Anchor delicate stems and leaves with pearl-headed sewing pins. Position the pins next to and slightly across the plant so that the pins won't show in the finished print.

FILM

There are several ways to anchor film to fabric. One is to cover the film with a piece of glass. Glass from a picture frame is readily available, but it is often very thin, has sharp edges, and breaks easily. For multiple prints, I suggest investing in 3/16"-window or 1/4"- thick plate glass. Request sanded edges to prevent cut fingers. For interesting effects, experiment with wire, etched, frosted, or even colored glass.

Just as the edge of a transparency will make a visible line on a blueprint, so will the edge of the glass. Avoid this problem by using a piece of glass that is larger than the print area or cover the glass edge with additional designs.

If printing conditions require that you prop up your design to orient it perpendicular to the sun, you will have to secure the glass to your base. This can be done by putting T-pins along the edges of the glass at an angle, making sure you pin all the way into the support base to hold the weight of the glass. Alternatively, you can make cel-

Secure glass to the support base with T-pins by placing the pins at an angle along all four sides of the glass, making sure you push the pins all the way into the base to hold the weight of the glass.

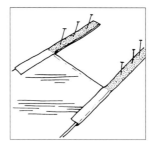

Secure glass to the support base with cellophane tape "suspenders" by sticking the tape to the sides of the glass, extending it far enough to clear the edge of the print, and pinning it to the support base.

lophane tape "suspenders" at the top of the glass and secure these to the base. Another option is to leave the glass in a picture frame and anchor the frame to the print. Adjustable clamps (not spring clamps) can also be used to hold the glass in place without stressing it. Be careful not to clamp the glass down too tightly or it may crack if it expands in the heat of the sun.

Glass intensifies sunlight exposure. Therefore, when working with glass on especially hot, bright days, reduce the exposure time. I suggest testing a range of exposure times from four minutes to ten minutes before beginning a printing project.

Another option is to anchor the film to the fabric with pearl-headed pins. Other pins will do, but I recommend pearl-headed pins because they are easy to remove once you've finished your print. Position the pins through the dense, dark areas of the film and push them all the way into the support to create a tight contact. Distribute the pins as evenly as possible across the entire surface of the image to create a uniform tight contact. You can reuse film that has been pinned if you're careful to put

the pins in the same holes each time—light can travel through pin holes and print unwanted dots. Ideally, you will print with a copy-machine duplicate and protect your original film.

Anchor film to the fabric by pushing pearl-headed pins through the dense, dark areas of the film and pushing them all the way into the support base to create a tight contact.

You can also use spray mount to secure film to fabric. It is sticky, messy, hard to work with, and can leave dot patterns on your work, but it is effective. It can be used where glass or hundreds of pins are not feasible, or on glass arrangements that will not have to be moved. I don't recommend it for repeated use on fabric with a nap or on knits such as T-shirts or sweat shirts—the fibers will adhere to the spray mount when the film is removed from the surface and obscure subsequent prints.

A wonderful product available at office, art, and graphic supply stores is repositionable design film. This transparent film is compatible with copy machines and laser printers. Because it is made to withstand the heat of these printers, it will also withstand the heat of the sun without buckling. It has a self-adhesive backing and will stay in place. It can be bought in individual sheets or in packages of ten. I suggest that you make a copy of your original composition onto a piece of repositionable design film. Then you can simply peel the film from the backing and stick it directly onto your fabric. Save the backing so that you can place the film back on it for storage between prints. As with spray mount, I do not recommend that you use this film repeatedly on fabric with a heavy nap.

PREPARING A GLASS PLATE FOR REPEAT PRINTING

Film or transparencies should be taped, spray mounted, or otherwise stuck to the bottom of the glass where they will be in direct contact with the fabric. Reeds, grasses, and other design elements can be taped to the top of the glass. You can get an interesting three-dimensional effect by putting

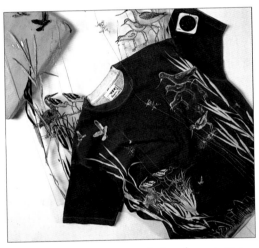

Use *cellophane tape* to secure design elements to a glass plate. Then place the plate on top of a pre-treated T-shirt mounted on a support base and expose for the desired length of time.

corners I attach cellophane tape "suspenders" reinforced with cotton tabs. I then push three $1^1/_2$"-long T-pins through each tab on a diagonal, pushing the pins all the way into the pinning board. These anchor pins carry the weight of the glass and hold it in place when the board is propped up in the sun.

If you are planning to print both the front and back of a garment, you can prepare one set-up for the front and a different set-up for the back to achieve a continuous design that encircles the garment.

LIGHTING FOR EXPOSURE

Before you set about printing, you need the right lighting conditions. If you want to make a series of prints, all with the same color, you'll need to print them all under similar time and light conditions.

design elements both on top of and beneath the glass. In the blueprint, the objects that were taped to the top of the glass will appear to be behind the images that were taped to the bottom.

I use 3/16"-thick window glass that is 22" by 28" and has sanded edges. To the top two

NATURAL SUNLIGHT

Sunlight is preferred over any type of artificial ultraviolet light. Because the sun is so far away, the source, as we experience it, is a single point of light.

For best results, print on a bright, clear, sunny day when there is no wind. The ideal temperature is 65–75°. Print midday (10 am to 3 pm), when the sun is directly overhead. Place the blueprint in full sunlight, stand back, and let the sun work its magic.

Because sunny locations change throughout the day, be aware of shadows created by trees, buildings, fences, and even overhead wires. The blueprint should be in full sunlight for the entire exposure time. Don't try to move your blueprint to keep it in the sun during exposure. The movement will cause the image to blur. Also consider the angle of the sun and position the blueprint perpendicular to the sun's rays. During sum-

Place the support board and mounted fabric perpindicular to the sun for exposure. Prop the support board if necessary.

mer months at noon, when the sun is directly overhead, the print can be placed flat on the ground. Earlier or later in the day, when the sun is lower in the sky, the print will have to be propped up to be perpendicular to the sun's rays.

It will take longer to achieve the same depth of blue on a print made during the winter on a clear, bright, sunny day than it will during the summer on a clear, bright, sunny day. When the temperature is above 80°F, decrease the exposure time. When the temperature is below 60°F, increase the exposure time. In extreme temperatures—over

95°F or below 50°F, try a test print.

For a successful blueprint, the light should be clear. A small amount of haze is tolerable as long as there are distinct shadows. The blueprint will not be affected by a few fast-moving clouds, but cloudy light, where the sun is alternately bright and dim, will require a longer exposure time to compensate for the time the light is reduced, and the print may blur while the sun is behind the clouds. Although any type of natural sunlight will expose a blueprint, the definition and intensity of color will suffer if the light is diffused or filtered as on a hazy day.

Prints will be overexposed if they are left out for half an hour or more in the sunlight, especially in hot weather. Overexposed prints will be a dark navy blue, and have a rusty-hazy look, and little or no design-print visible. A portrait, for example, would have obscured features and the print would be mostly blue with little contrast.

Prints will be underexposed if they are left out only two or three minutes on a clear, bright, sunny day. Underexposed prints are pale blue with little or no visible design or image. They look faded or washed-out.

ARTIFICIAL LIGHT

Although the clearest prints are made by the sun on warm, clear days, you can also expose blueprints under artificial ultraviolet lights. Because there are so many factors affecting the intensity of artificial lights, it is always a good idea to experiment with scraps of pretreated fabric before doing a project. Use only dry fabric as wet fabric does not dry well under artificial light, and try an initial exposure time of ten minutes.

ULTRAVIOLET LIGHT

Ultraviolet (UV) florescent light tubes in

the 300 to 360 nanometer range, commonly called black lights, will also expose blueprints. These are rather expensive and care must be taken not to look directly at them as eyes may be damaged. Extensive exposure to ultraviolet light will cause "sun burn" effects on the skin. Sunglasses that filter out UV light, sunscreen lotions, long sleeves, and gloves will minimize these potential hazards.

Ultraviolet light tubes are available in 18" and 48" lengths and can be ordered from a lighting specialist. They can be inserted and used in a standard two-tube florescent light fixture available at building supply stores. Always use a grounded utility extension cord plugged into a grounded outlet.

If you plan to use UV light tubes, you must build a box to hold the light fixtures and to shield your eyes. Build a box that is 2" bigger on the inside than the overall size of the light fixtures. Mount the light fixtures

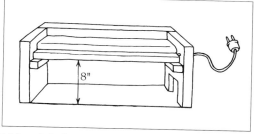

Make a light box 2" bigger on the inside than the overall size of the light fixture that holds UV light tubes. There should be 8" between the base of the light tubes and the floor.

on a strip of wood glued or nailed to the sides of the box. There should be about 8" of clearance between the base of the light tubes and the floor. You can leave an opening on one end or one side through which to slide prints in and out. Cover the opening with light-proof black plastic. The usual exposure time is ten minutes.

UV light boxes that are used to expose screen printing emulsions will also expose blueprints. In these boxes, the lights are usually mounted on the floor of the box and the top is covered with glass. Therefore, they are only practical with flat design sources such as film, cut paper, lacework, etc. The design source is positioned on the glass, the fabric is taped in place over it, a foam pad and weight are placed over it to ensure tight contact, and everything is covered with light-proof cloth or plastic before the lights are turned on. If you are using a light box with a vacuum seal, weights are not necessary.

The disadvantage of light boxes is that the light tubes produce an even field of light Since light surrounds the design source, the resulting print will be a bit blurred. The size of the project is greatly limited as it can be only as big as the box.

MERCURY ARC LAMPS

You can also expose blueprints under mercury arc lamps. These are electric lamps in which the discharge of light takes place through mercury vapor in an arc. Mercury arc lamps are very expensive and must be housed in special containers which can be heavy and difficult to manage. Always use total protective eye and skin covering when the light is turned on, and use the light only in a darkroom situation.

A mercury arc lamp works well because, like the sun, it is a single point of light. The radius of the light and the distance that the print is from the source will affect the color of the blueprint. The intensity of the blue color in the blueprint will be increased if the treated fabric is placed close to the light. On larger prints, where the design extends beyond the radius of light, the intensity of the blue color will fade out. This shading can produce some beautiful effects and should not be overlooked as a design objective.

SUN LAMPS

I don't recommend using sun lamps for

blueprinting. They are no longer manufactured because of the skin and eye damage they have caused. Any lamps that may still exist are too old and unpredictable to be considered safe.

TANNING SALONS OR HOME TANNING LIGHT TUBES

These are just like the ultraviolet florescent light tubes already discussed, and the same precautions apply. The lights are usually mounted on a curved surface to encompass 50% to 100% of the body. A design source and pinning board will be surrounded in light as well and the resulting print will probably be blurred.

TIMING FOR EXPOSURE

In general, hot, sunny, summer days call for five to ten minutes of exposure; cool, bright, spring and fall days eight to fifteen minutes; and cold, clear, winter days fifteen to twenty minutes. Heavier fabrics need the longest exposure times in all cases.

It's always a good idea to test for the exposure time. You could expose many different pieces of pretreated fabric for many different time periods, or you could go about it in a more structured way, using a single piece of fabric. Pin a piece of treated fabric 10" long by at least 4" wide to a support. Pin a design element across the fabric along the full length to protect some of the fabric from exposure so you will be able to observe contrasts in the print color. Cover all but a 2" segment with a piece of light-proof cardboard. Every two minutes, move the cardboard 2" to expose another segment of fabric. Remove the fabric from the base, rinse it well and let it dry. The different colors represent the different exposure times.

By duplicating a particular exposure time, you can achieve the color you want. You can even remove some design objects part way through the exposure time to get a variety of colors in a single piece. If you plan to print wet fabric, use wet fabric for your tests.

BLUEPRINTING WET FABRIC

Many people derive great satisfaction from each step of producing an art piece. So do I, but I love shortcuts; that's how I discovered this wet-fabric printing technique. I read about the blueprint process using the traditional method of drying the fabric and exposing it to sunlight using film as the design source. I am a fabric designer, and unfortunately have no photography experience. When I began blueprinting, I had no darkroom, no convenient place to dry fabric, and no film. I had never taken a

Test different exposure times. Shown here are natural raw silk, white rayon, white cotton, fuchsia cotton, and turquoise cotton. From top to bottom, the fabrics are unexposed, exposed for 2, 4, 6, 8, 10, and 12 minutes.

photography course nor read any photographic history. I did not even know about contact printing, but I assumed that anything that blocked light would leave an impression.

What I did have was a garden, a sunny yard, and a desire to try this process. In my garage I painted the blueprint formula solution onto natural-colored cotton muslin. Then I went outside and pulled some vegetables from the garden—roots and all—, pinned them on the treated fabric and immediately began printing in the driveway. The fabric was wet and fresh from the paint brush, and I watched it dry in the hot Texas sun. It worked just fine, and I thus discovered the advantages of wet fabric printing—ease and speed. The fabric can also be painted in place on a support base, the design pinned on, and the entire unit taken directly out into the sun.

It is best to print wet fabric in warm weather. Images become blurry if exposed longer than fifteen or twenty minutes, but this may not be a long enough time for the fabric to dry even in bright sun on a cool day. If the exposed part of the fabric does not dry completely, the damp areas will turn a different color (most commonly purple on

For blueprinting wet fabric, pin the design elements directly onto the wet fabric.

a blue-and-white print) and the edges of the image may be fuzzy.

The weight, size, and texture of the design source will affect how well the fabric dries. Heavy objects, large branches, or dense leaves will slow evaporation and prevent drying close to the edges or between

Prop the mounted fabric and design so that it is perpindicular to the sun.

elements. For example, a crocheted piece made of heavy yarn would require more

drying time than a fine thread or lace pattern that allows considerable light and air between the spaces. The evaporation process can actually be observed in the sunlight as the fabric dries—in summer, wet fabric exposure usually takes from eight to twelve minutes. Leave the print in the sun until the fabric has dried up to the edges of the design elements. The color will change as the fabric dries—from the original yellow-green to a hazy, blue-grey. The characteristic bright, Prussian blue will appear *only* after the fabric has been rinsed in water.

If you want some color variation, deliberately move the design elements during exposure. Begin by letting the fabric completely dry to the edge of the design element, then move the element and expose for another two minutes. Do not use glass or film of any kind on wet fabric.

BLUEPRINTING DRY FABRIC

Blueprinting dry fabric allows more freedom in choosing design sources, is cleaner to work with than wet fabric, and is not susceptible to cool weather's limited drying and evaporation capabilities.

Because dry fabric does not exhibit the instantly dramatic color changes during exposure that wet fabric does, it is essential that exposures be timed. Do not rely on visual interpretation alone. The bright, Prussian blue color will not appear until after the print has been rinsed. Clothing and hemmed or multilayered fabric should be dry when printed to achieve an even color.

Dry fabric can be exposed in cool climates as long as the sun conditions are bright and clear and the subject is oriented perpendicular to the sun's rays.

The same conditions apply for dry and wet fabric when moving the design elements during exposure. After the initial exposure time, move some design elements, if desired, and continue the exposure at least two more minutes to ensure color development in the newly exposed areas.

EXPOSING FILM ON DRY FABRIC

As always, test prints are recommended. The best prints are achieved when care is taken to ensure a tight film-fabric contact and the print is positioned perpendicular to the sun. During exposure time, do not move either the film or the support board unless you want to end up with a blurred image.

FIXING THE EXPOSED BLUEPRINT

You are almost ready to view your artwork! Once the pretreated fabric has been exposed for the desired length of time, move it inside, away from direct light, and remove the design sources. The areas that have been exposed to light will be a hazy blue or blue-grey. The areas that were covered by design objects will be the same shade of yellow-green they were before exposure. Areas that were partially exposed or in shadow during exposure will be a darker shade of green or a tone of blue.

Now the print needs to be rinsed thoroughly in clean water for the blue-and-white image to become visible. Rinsing will turn the hazy blue to vivid blue, and the yellow-green will return to white. Tap water is usually acceptable, but if your water supply is high in mineral content, use distilled or bottled water or water that has been processed through a filter, conditioner, or

After the fabric has been exposed for the desired length of time, move it inside away from direct light, remove the design sources, and remove the fabric from the support base.

water softener for the final rinse.

You can rinse your blueprint by hand or by machine. This is a matter of choice, but large pieces are generally easier to rinse in a machine and small pieces by hand. A clean bathtub can also be used for large pieces, but be sure to rinse out any soap or cleanser residue before you put the blueprint in the tub.

HAND RINSING

Rubber gloves should be used during this step so that your hands won't get stained. Fill a sink or basin with enough clean water to completely cover your print. Use a clean sink that is free of cleansers. Avoid using a darkroom sink where other chemicals (acids) may cause secondary reactions. Submerge the print and rinse, swishing it back and forth vigorously to remove all of the unbonded solution. The water will turn green as the unexposed chemicals are rinsed out. Drain this water and rinse again. Continue rinsing and draining until the rinse water remains clear.

MACHINE RINSING

The advantage of machine rinsing is that you can rinse up to six yards of fabric at one time. First, clean the washing machine inside and out to remove any soap residue that might change the color of your blueprint to

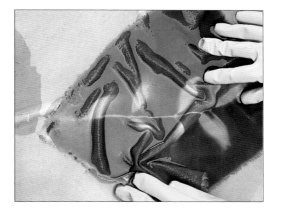

With gloved hands, submerge the print in clean water and swish it vigorously to remove all of the unbonded solution. Drain the rinse water and repeat with clean water until the rinse water remains uncolored.

yellow or green (see "Removing the Blue Color", page 64). Clean the machine by running at least one rinse cycle with hot water. After the machine is clean, run your fabric through a complete wash, rinse, and extra rinse cycle using cold water—but don't use soap or your blueprint may disappear! Because of a machine's agitation, a long piece of fabric can get twisted into a "rope" which prevents thorough rinsing. If raveled threads from the raw edges wind around the cloth, a "tie-dyed" look will result. Be sure to check for these occurrences during the rinse cycle and redistribute the fabric in the machine as necessary. If the fabric seems stiff at the end of the cycle, run it through another rinse. (Rayon always will be stiff after rinsing—it will soften only after it's dry.)

The majority of the chemicals used in printing will have bonded to the fabric during exposure (the blue part); the unexposed chemicals will rinse out and be flushed down the drain with the wash and rinse water (usually sixteen gallons per extra-large load).

SPECIAL CONSIDERATIONS

If your fabric was printed wet, the areas that were under design elements may not have dried completely during exposure, especially if printed in cool weather. After rinsing, these areas may appear purple and mottled. If this happens, wash a small print in a basin with 1/2 teaspoon of liquid hand soap, or a large print in a washing machine with 1/8 cup of liquid, non-phosphate soap. This treatment may help brighten and clear the blotchy areas. Rinse well to remove all of the soap. (See "Washing", page 68.)

If you've used treated fabric that has been stored for some time—six months to five years—it probably will have oxidized to

Two finished prints. The shadowy outlines on the leaf at top were created by moving the leaves during exposure, allowing sunlight to reach the fabric below them.

some degree and turned dark green or blue. When it is rinsed out after exposure, it may produce a blue-on-blue print, rather than blue background with a bright white print. Follow the initial rinse with a light soap wash as described above and rinse again to help sharpen the color contrast.

DRYING THE BLUEPRINTS

Dry blueprints inside, away from direct sunlight. Although a print is fixed as a result of the rinsing, direct sunlight on a wet, freshly rinsed print can cause brown- or rust-colored streaks. This is most probably the result of insufficient rinsing. If this happens, wash the print again using a little non-phosphate liquid soap. Rinse well and dry inside.

Small prints can be dried on a counter or table covered with newspaper or paper towels. After rinsing, squeeze out excess water and lay the prints out to dry. If you notice a blue color on the drying pad, the prints have not been thoroughly rinsed. Immediately rinse again. If you're in a hurry, you can speed up the drying time by using a hair dryer or small heater.

Large pieces can be hung from a pant hanger or a clean clothesline to dry. Hang the print so that it extends down from the line rather than folding it over the line.

You can dry up to six yards of fabric at a time in a clothes dryer. Set the temperature appropriately for the fabric—cotton on high for thirty minutes; silk on low for fifteen. Remove the fabric promptly to avoid setting wrinkles.

COLOR
VARIATIONS

For years I exhibited my printed clothing at art shows and I rarely saw anyone else using this technique. I was known as "The Blueprint Lady". My booth was filled with a huge variety of styles and prints; each year we produced new selections in my studio. We exchanged ideas for visual puns and delighted in new designs to surprise the mind and the spirit—chicken wire jackets, pasta and popcorn jumpers, tools and screws and nails, underwater fantasies, butterflies and flowers, dream windows, hummingbirds and dinosaurs. Maps, politics, and Victorian houses also had their moments. Nothing was overlooked, everything was worth trying.

Then, in the booth one day, I heard a voice ask, "Do you have anything besides blue?"

That set us off on exciting experiments with color that opened up a new world of possibilities. It's a bit like cooking; one ingredient affects another. Substitute colored fabrics for white. Surprise yourself.

When the blueprint solution is applied to colored fabrics, secondary colors result from the blue blending with the original color. The same color-mixing principals used for blending paints or dyes apply to blueprinting. The initial color composition of the fabric will influence the blueprinted results.

The initial color of a fabric will influence the blueprinted results. Shown here from left to right are blueprints on light-blue silk, turquoise silk, and fuchsia silk.

A blueprint solution applied to natural raw silk will produce an off-white print on a blue-green field. A turquoise fabric will yield a turquoise print on a dark blue background. Fuchsia yields a fuchsia print on a purple field, and pink fabric set at a three-minute exposure will give a pink print on a lavender field.

The possibilities are as varied as the shades of colors that are available. By varying the time of exposure from three to twenty minutes, a wide range of color intensity can be achieved. You can even expose different sections of the same print for varying time periods to create multiple effects.

You can use hand-dyed fabrics as a base for blueprinting. Dyed fabrics should be washed well to remove excess dye and dried before being treated for blueprinting. Excess dye in the fabric can leach out into the blueprint solution as it is applied and may dark-

Blueprints on blue and pink silk.

en and change the blueprint formula. The resulting print will be a muddy, disappointing color with little contrast. Because many hand-dying processes require salt and/or soda to fix the dye, always dye the fabric *before* you blueprint it. If the fabric is dyed after blueprinting, these substances will pull the blue color out of the print.

REMOVING THE BLUE COLOR: YELLOW-AND-WHITE PRINTS

There are many substances that will remove the blue color in a blueprint: ammonium hydroxide (often mentioned in alternative photographic methods), chlorine bleach, hydrogen peroxide, phosphate-based soap, sodium metasilicate, sodium silicate, sodium sulfate, tri-sodium phosphate (TSP), and washing or baking soda. Substances that contain sodium or phosphate are present in many granular laundry soaps. Chlorine bleach is hard on fabrics and has disagreeable fumes and odors. Ammonium hydroxide is not a household product. It is unpleasant, difficult to work with, and should only be used in a chemistry or photo laboratory with proper equipment, vents, and hoods.

The fastest and easiest way to remove the

In addition to shades of blue, yellow and brown prints are also possible. Shown here are blue, yellow, and brown prints each on raw silk (top three) and cotton (bottom three).

blue is to use TSP. Though packaged as tri-sodium phosphate, it may contain sodium metasilicate. TSP is a strong cleanser and grease remover often used to wash walls prior to painting. It is available at building supply centers and paint stores.

Wearing rubber gloves, mix TSP in a

bucket using hot tap water to dissolve the granules and then cool water for comfort. Mix the solution in a glass or plastic container and use plastic sticks or spoons to stir.

Prepare enough solution to completely submerge the print. The amount of TSP to use depends on the quantity of fabric being treated. For several small prints, for example, six 8" squares, use one tablespoon TSP dissolved in one quart of water. Three yards of fabric will probably need one-half cup of TSP to four gallons of water. If the fabric is particularly heavy or very dark blue, one cup of TSP will be needed. After using the solution for several prints, the solution may become exhausted and unable to pull the blue out of the fabric effectively. Simply dissolve more TSP in hot water and add it to the first solution, stirring thoroughly.

Once the blue color is removed, rinse the yellow print well in clean water. Several rinses will be needed to thoroughly remove the TSP from the fabric. Large fabric pieces can be rinsed in a full wash cycle in a washing machine without adding soap. I do not recommend introducing TSP solution into the washing machine. It is difficult to dissolve and could leave a residue that might cause spots on the next load of laundry or blueprint fabric.

The resulting yellow-and-white print is permanent. Nothing I have tested has been able to remove the yellow. Depending upon the original shade of blue, the yellow will vary from pale yellow to golden yellow.

BROWN-TONING BLUEPRINTS

Brown-toning a blueprint is an easy two-step process. The results mimic the color of a sepia print or a Van Dyke brownprint, but these photographic methods are entirely dif-

Brown-tone prints, which resemble sepia or Van Dyke brownprints, are produced by removing the blue color and then applying tannic acid.

ferent processes. In a brown-toned blueprint, the quality and depth of brown is directly related to the quality and depth of blue in the original blueprint. All of the shades of blue will be represented in shades of brown. The white areas will not be as bright as they originally were, but they will keep their integrity. Brown-toning is easy and fun; it's "kitchen chemistry".

The first step is to remove the blue color from the blueprint (see above), resulting in a yellow-and-white print. The second step is to apply tannic acid to tone the yellow areas brown.

Tannic acid is found in dark woods, red wine, and dark teas, and it can be purchased from chemical suppliers. For small projects, Lipton's Orange Pekoe & Pekoe Cut Black Tea is an inexpensive, easy-to-obtain source of tannic acid. (Green and herbal teas do not contain tannic acid.)

Bring two cups of water to a boil, add eight to ten tea bags, and steep approximately ten minutes until the color is a rich, dark brown. Remove the tea bags. Agitate the yellow print in the tea bath until the yellow areas absorb the brown color. This solution will be enough to do several small prints. When the prints no longer turn brown, add freshly brewed tea. After toning, rinse the prints in clean water and dry. For a darker brown, use a more concentrated tea bath.

For large or on-going projects, I suggest buying tannic acid from a chemical supplier rather than using dozens of tea bags. Besides convenience, one pound of tannic acid will tone at least ten yards of 54"-wide fabric. Because tannic acid is powdered, it drifts in the air. Therefore, cover your work area with newspapers and wear a dust mask. Everything the acid comes in contact with

will stain brown, so wear rubber gloves and protective or old clothing. The brown tint can be removed from a print or other object where it is undesired with bleach.

To make enough solution to process three yards of 54"-wide cotton sheeting, put about one cup of tannic acid in a plastic or glass container and slowly add tap water, about two gallons. The tannic acid will become sticky when it comes in contact with water; add the water slowly, as if making a roux. Stir thoroughly until the tannic acid is dissolved. If you need more acid to intensify the color, dissolve it first in a small container and then add it to the larger solution.

Because brown-toning is a tint and not a dye, repeated washing will cause the brown color to fade. The color can usually be restored by making a fresh solution of tannic acid and dipping the print again.

CARE OF BLUEPRINTED FABRIC

WASHING

Blueprints can be washed and will look wonderful for many years if properly cared for. Water temperature does not seem to be important for maintaining the print, so choose the water temperature appropriate for the fabric.

Because there are so many laundry products available, it is important to understand which ingredients to avoid. The same substances I mentioned in the section on removing the blue color from a print are the ones to avoid when washing a blueprint—they will cause the blue to turn yellow or yellow-green: ammonium hydroxide, chlorine bleach, hydrogen peroxide, sodium metasilicate, sodium silicate, sodium sulfate, tri-sodium phosphate (TSP), and washing or baking soda. Commercial powdered products to avoid using for washing blueprints include: Arm & Hammer,

Clorox I, Clorox II, Comet cleanser, Ivory Snow, Tide, and 20 Mule Team Borax. In fact, I do not recommend using powdered soap of any kind, not even biodegradable brands (most biodegradable products contain washing soda). Powdered soaps do not uniformly dissolve. Undissolved powdered soap granules will cause spots to form on a blueprint. If you are presently using powdered soap in your washing machine, it will be necessary to rinse out all soap residues with a hot-water cycle before washing your blueprints. Don't wash blueprints in public laundromats or commercial laundries—their equipment is commonly caked with undissolved soap.

I do recommend liquid hand and dish products such as Dove, Ivory, Joy, and Palmolive, and liquid laundry soaps such as Clout, Tide, Wisk, and Woolite. Always test products using a blueprinted swatch. I have not tested shampoos, but suspect that they may be safe as well.

For hand washing, say, one shirt, use 1/2 teaspoon soap per basin. For machine washing, use 1/4 cup soap per large tub of clothes. First dissolve the soap in the water, then add the blueprint. Do not soak the print—it could float unevenly on the surface, possibly resulting in visible soap rings. After washing, line dry inside or dry in a dryer set for the appropriate fabric temperature.

If you get a spot on your blueprint, remove it with a product designed to be a spot remover. Do not use undiluted soap—it will cause a blueprint to fade. Rit Grease and Stain Remover #90 works well. Whatever you use, there will be less chance of fading if you apply the spot remover to the back of the print and then rinse thoroughly. Read labels carefully and test the product on a blueprint scrap before using.

The blueprint color is stable only if these soap recommendations are followed. And always use the minimum amount of soap—too much soap will fade the print. If a blueprint is accidently washed in a soap that changes the color, follow the steps for a yellow or brown print. You may like it just as well.

DRY CLEANING

Some dry cleaning methods work well on blueprints. To avoid possible problems, take blueprint swatches to the cleaner for testing. Use a dry cleaning establishment that does the work on the premises—that way you can talk directly to the person actually doing the work. Some dry cleaning spot removers will remove the blue color. Make sure these are tested as well before use.

IRONING

A blueprint will change color when a hot iron is applied. After the fabric cools, the color will return to its original blue shade.

Set the iron temperature appropriately for the fabric. Use a good-quality steam iron or a dry iron and a spray bottle. A leaky steam iron may cause water spots.

SPECIAL CONSIDERATIONS

A blueprint is just that, a print. It is not a dye that penetrates the fiber; it affects only the surface of the fabric. Repeated washing and drying causes surface fibers to wear off resulting in lint. As the surface is worn away, the blue appears to fade. The more gently the fabric is handled, the less it will "fade". A hand-washed and indoor line-dried blueprint will retain better color than one that is machine-washed and tumble-dried.

Leaving a blueprint in direct sun for a long period of time will cause some fading, but it will not harm the print. As a test in our studio, we cut a blueprint in half and for one week, one half was kept inside while the other was left outside in full sun. When we brought the "outside" half back inside, the blue color was considerably lighter than the "inside" one. We kept both pieces inside overnight, and the next morning, they were the same color! We had to check our notes on the backs of the prints to determine which one was which. Sunlight affects the color of fabric the same as heat from an iron does. Extreme heat will change the color, but once conditions stabilize, so does the color.

Soda—baking soda (bicarbonate of soda)—is sometimes added to soaps and deodorants as an antiperspirant. Soda is on the list of things not to use on blueprints because it will remove the blue color. A deodorant containing soda could cause yellow patches under the arms of a blueprinted shirt. Salty perspiration could have the same effect. Once the blue color has been lost, there is no way to restore it evenly. So, once again, read labels carefully so that you'll get the longest possible enjoyment out of your blueprint.

The yellowish blotches in this T-shirt were caused by accidental contact with powered laundry detergent. However, note that the image remains even though the color has changed.

PROJECTS

CHILE PEPPER
T-SHIRT

A garland of chile peppers makes for a bold and exciting shirt. If this hot theme doesn't suit your tastes, consider garlands of herbs, hearts, flowers, or stars.

Each year I collect chile pepper and other herb garlands—garlic, bay leaves, etc.—to use for cooking, decoration, and blueprinting. If care is taken, these garlands can be reused many times for printing and eventually added to the soup pot. Backyard gardens offer an abundance of suitable vegetables and herbs to choose from.

For this project you'll need a red T-shirt; design source; support board a little larger than the shirt; pearl-headed sewing pins; black plastic or a heavy paper bag.

I began with a red, 100% cotton T-shirt, washed and rinsed it in hot water to remove the sizing, and dried it in a household drier. Next, I submerged the shirt in the blueprint solution, wrung out the excess chemicals (through an electric wringer), and dried the shirt in a household dryer. See pages 20–27 for details on these steps or purchase a pre-treated shirt. Store the prepared shirt in a light-proof bag until you are ready to print.

A note here about color. The shade of red in this shirt contains some yellow. Therefore, during the blueprinting process, all

three primary colors—red, yellow, and blue—are present, resulting in a dark, charcoal brown background print that appears almost black. The chile images retain the original red color of the shirt.

Printing a T-shirt is a reasonably big project that warrants some planning. Although some of these suggestions may sound trivial, the seemingly insignificant details can greatly influence the final appearance of the shirt.

T-shirts are constructed from unstructured tubes of cotton knit. After the factory sizing is removed (a necessary step in blueprinting), a T-shirt loses its shape. You may find getting a T-shirt to lie flat on a support board to be a challenge.

Working downward from the neck, use pearl-headed sewing pins to pin the neck, shoulders, and sleeves to the support board. Then put one hand inside the shirt and smooth the wrinkles out and down from the

inside while holding the hem with the other hand. When all of the wrinkles have been smoothed out, pin the sides and hem as straight as possible. Take your time and pay close attention—wrinkles in the fabric will print as lines and blobs that will interfere with the design. If one side of the shirt is pinned and printed smoothly, there will be few wrinkles to smooth out when the shirt is turned over to print the other side, and the exposure and color will be even all the way to the edges.

When printing the front, use a piece of black plastic or heavy paper to cover the fabric exposed at the neck opening and prevent it from printing. For a fun surprise, after finishing the outside, turn the shirt inside out and print a design on the inside as well.

A T-shirt requires a large support base that will have to be held nearly vertical to get through a doorway. Make sure that your design element—the pepper garland in this case—is secured well enough that it won't sag or fall off during transport. To pin the

Anchor the garland in place with pins. Cross and lock the heads of the pins on one another as shown. Use only sewing or quilt pins. Large T-pins make holes in T-shirts.

pepper garland to the shirt, cross and lock two pearl-headed sewing pins over the cord that strings the peppers together. Push the pins as far down into the support as possible so that they will not show in the print. Put pairs of crossed pins every two or three inches to hold the garland in place.

The next step is to take the mounted shirt

assembly outside, position it perpendicular to the sun, and expose it to the sunlight for the desired number of minutes.

After exposure is complete (usually 10 to 15 minutes for T-shirts), take the shirt assembly inside. Unpin the pepper garland and the shirt, turn the shirt over, and smooth it out. Allow just a little bit (1/4") of the printed side to show around all of the edges so that there will be no negative (unprinted) lines along the shoulder, sleeves, and sides.

Pin the garland to the back of the shirt, aligning the peppers at the shoulders so that the print continues uninterrupted from front to back.

Return the composition outdoors and expose it for the same amount of time as you did for the front. Remember, the sun will have moved some and you may need to adjust your exposure angle.

Finally, bring the shirt inside, remove the peppers and pins, rinse the shirt thoroughly, and let it dry. The final color will deepen and the contrasts sharpen as the shirt dries.

CIRCLE T-SHIRT

This type of mini print offers a quick, fun approach for special events or group activities. A special gift shirt can be uniquely personalized. Commemorative souvenirs can be printed at a family or class reunion. For children's parties, blueprinting circle shirts can be an activity that produces party favors. Should you want all the shirts blueprinted in a group activity to be alike, use a design source that can be photocopied. Then make several copies of the design onto adhesive-back transparency film for the group to share.

For this project you will need a pretreated circle T-shirt; design source; support board; piece of glass larger than the design source; pearl-headed sewing pins.

Although you can purchase T-shirts with circles pretreated for blueprinting, it's easy to prepare one yourself. Cover a support board (a sturdy box or piece of foam board about $8^{1}/_{2}$" × 11" is adequate) with two layers of black-and-white newspaper. Place the covered board inside the shirt and use pearl-head sewing pins to pin the shirt snugly

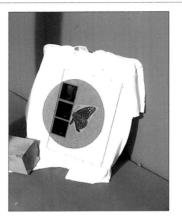

around the edge of the board. Paint the blueprinting solution on the shirt. Make a circle stencil by cutting the appropriate size circle out of a piece of heavy paper or mat board. Place the mat board over the shirt with the hole centered as desired.

You can print the shirt while the solution is still wet if you plan to use natural or other non-precious objects. Just let the exposed, wet area dry completely in the sun. You can speed the drying time by replacing the wet paper covering the support board with dry paper before exposure. If you want to use film as a design source, you must dry the painted area first. Remove the T-shirt from the board and allow it to dry completely (a hair dryer works well to speed drying time), then replace the board, and arrange the design.

For the shirt shown here, I used a black-and-white strip negative film and a draw-ing of a butterfly that had been photocopied onto adhesive-back transparency film. Because I was using film, the pretreated shirt had to be completely dried before beginning. (For details on working with film and transparencies, see pages 44–47). I positioned the strip negative and covered it with a piece of glass (from a picture frame) to form a uniform tight contact. Knowing that the sun was positioned at an angle in the sky and that the assembly would have to be propped up for exposure, I placed sewing pins along all four sides of the glass to hold it in place. I then peeled the backing off the transparency film and firmly pressed the butterfly image in place onto the blueprint-treated area.

Expose the shirt assembly perpendicular to the sun for the desired time, remove the design elements, and rinse the shirt thoroughly by placing the blueprinted area face down in a basin filled with water and agitating it vigorously. Change the rinse water and repeat the process until the water remains clear. To prevent the blueprint solution from tracking onto the white, untreated areas of the shirt, avoid squeezing or wringing the shirt until you are certain that it has been thoroughly rinsed. Hang the shirt to line dry indoors away from direct sunlight.

P I L L O W

Blueprints make appealing memory prints. And it seems appropriate to use a historic printing process to reproduce old pictures. Old photographs are ideal for blueprinting because the images are typically of high quality. Before Kodak introduced its Brownie Box camera, most family pictures were taken by traveling photographers. For these events, family members gathered in their best clothes, and lights and seating were arranged for formal portraits. These well-composed images make charming cyanotypes.

This pillow has old-fashioned charm, but the materials are all new. The instructions are for a pillow with finished dimensions of 15" × 17", but you could make adjustments to fit any pillow size.

For this project you'll need a pretreated 8" × 8" cloth square; negative or other design element; support board; glass to cover the design source; pearl-headed sewing pins; 12" × 14" light-colored complementary fabric; 1/4 yard of darker colored complementary fabric; 1 yard of lace; 2 yards of piping; 14" × 16" pillow form; scissors; sewing machine.

Secure the pretreated cotton fabric to the support base with pins. Place the design element on the fabric and secure it in place. (See pages 44–47 for complete instructions for printing film.) Put the fabric in the sunlight for the desired exposure time, rinse thoroughly, and dry.

The blueprint is framed by lace and two fabric borders for the pillow front.

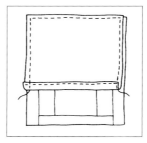

Stitch one of the back pieces to the front, right sides together.

Cut four 4"-wide strips of light-colored fabric and sew them to the edges of the print, forming a border. On top of this border, outline the print with lace, mitering the corners. Cut four 3"-wide strips of dark fabric and sew these to the outer edges of the light fabric border.

For the back of the pillow, cut two pieces of the darker fabric, each 15" × 12". Hem each along one of the 15" edges. (These hemmed edges will overlap in the back to cover the opening through which the pillow form will be inserted.) With right sides together, pin one of the back pieces to the

Stitch the second back piece to the front, right sides together, and over-lapping the other back piece.

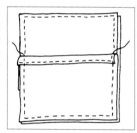

front, lining up the edges and with the finished edge lying across the center of the pillow front. Stitch in place with a 1/2" seam allowance. Position the second piece of dark fabric so that the edges line up with those of the other half of the pillow front and the finished edge overlaps the finished edge of the other half-back. Stitch in place with a 1/2" seam allowance. Trim seam allowances and turn the work right-side-out.

To make a casing for piping, cut 2"-wide strips of the lighter fabric, enough to make one 2-yard strip. Stitch them together end to end to make a single piece of fabric. With

right sides together, stitch the casing to the front of the pillow case with a 1/4" seam allowance. Bring the casing around to the back, turn under the cut edge, and topstitch in place around all four sides, folding back the raw edge where the two ends of the border meet. Slide the piping through the casing and slipstitch the edges of the casing together. Slide a pillow form through the slit in the back. Voila!

PHOTO ALBUM OR BOOK COVER

Photo album covers are ideal for showcasing photo blueprints. The instructions here are for covering a 7" × 9" photo album that is $1^1/_2$" thick, but the techniques can be used for any size book or album. This is a simple project that can be dressed up with quilting, lace, or other embellishments.

For this project you'll need a piece of pre-

treated cloth that is 2" wider and 8" longer than the book when opened (9" × 23.5" in this case); support board; pearl-headed sewing pins; scissors; sewing machine; 7" × 9" photo album.

Find the center of the pretreated cloth, allow for the width of the binding, and center design source in the space on the front (and on the back, if desired). Print in the usual way, rinse, dry, and iron.

Fold under 1/2" on all four sides and iron flat. Fold under $1^1/_4$" on the top and bottom edges, and $3^1/_4$" under on each side— this will form the book flaps. Press in place, topstitch 1/8" from all edges, and put the cover on your album or book.

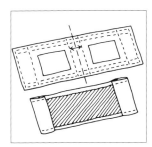

Construct the album cover by folding under a seam on all four sides, folding under a facing on the top and bottom edges, and then folding over the two side edges to make book flaps.

FAUX QUILT

A faux quilt may never become an heirloom, but it may well become a treasured keepsake. It's easier than it looks and it's fun.

For this project you'll need a piece of pre-quilted, natural fiber fabric (you could also use unquilted fabic and quilt it yourself after printing) measuring 108" × 54" (pure cotton works best, but you could substitute a cotton/polyester blend that contains at least 50 percent cotton); blueprinting solution; design source; support board; pearl-head-ed sewing pins; 1^1/$_2$ yards of white silk charmeuse for the border; a few pieces of string or rubberbands; a 2"-wide strip of polyester batting 9 yards long (enough to go completely around the quilt); 9 yards red silk cording; scissors; sewing machine.

I prepared my quilted fabric for blueprinting by submerging it in a large tub and running it through the wringer of an old-fashioned washing machine. The fabric was very heavy and I needed help to balance the weight; one person fed it through the wringer, the other received it. I printed the piece wet.

If you want to print a heavy, wet piece like this, you should to do it on a hot, summer day. Of course, you can choose to print it dry under less optimum conditions but it will take considerably longer. I chose branches and leaves from a large, blue eucalyptus tree that had leaves averaging 12" in length. During the last two minutes of

Blueprint a "tie-dyed" effect by folding pre-treated fabric in 2"-3" pleats and secure them with ties. then expose the bundle to sunlight. Refold and retie it several times to expose new areas.

exposure on the first side, I moved the leaves to get some color variation. Then I brought the piece inside, turned it over, took it back outside, and printed the other side. Following exposure, I rinsed the print thoroughly through two complete extra-large wash cycles in a clean washing machine. The bulky fabric and large quantity of chemical in this piece required a lot of rinsing. During the rinse cycles, I lifted and shifted the fabric frequently to ensure thorough and uniform rinsing.

For the binding, print about 1½ yards of white silk charmeuse with the following "tie-dyed" technique to produce an ab-

stract line design. First treat the silk with the blueprint solution and allow it to dry. Then fold the entire length of the fabric in 2"–3" pleats (they do not have to be even, regular folds) and tie around the fabric (you could use rubber bands) in several places. Expose the bundle to bright sunlight for ten minutes. Then bring the bundle inside, refold it to expose new areas, retie it, and expose it for another 10 minutes. Repeat the process three or four times, and then fold and expose the width of the fabric in the same manner, three or four times. Rinse and dry the fabric.

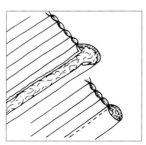

Sew one dege of the binding to the quilt, right sides together, place strips of polyester batting on the wrong side of the binding, fold the binding over the batting, and stitch it to the other side of the quilt.

Cut the tie-printed fabric into 4" binding strips and then sew the strips together end to end to make a piece long enough to encircle the quilt. Fold under and press 1/4" on both sides of the strip. Sew one edge of the binding to the quilt, right sides together. Then place strips of polyester batting (cut to half the width of the binding) on the wrong side of the binding, fold the binding over the batting, and machine top stitch the other edge of the binding, with the folded edge inside, to the other side of the quilt. Hand sew red silk cording on top of the binding stitch for a bright, contrasting accent.

GARDEN VARIETY BLANKET

I've always enjoyed reading about herb, vegetable, and flower gardens. I imagine colors and fragrances and fantasize about the heady rewards of tilling soil. I've even gotten as far as purchasing seeds at my local

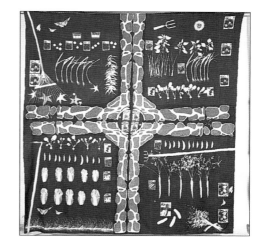

garden center. But I never seem to find time to plant the seeds in my garden bed.

So, I decided to use the seed packets to make my bed into a garden by printing garden images on a white flannel blanket.

For this blueprinted garden you'll need a king-sized white flannel sheet; 16-gallon tub of blueprint solution; seed packets and other garden theme design elements; support board; pins; white paper; black felt-

Detail of the Garden Variety Blanket.

print garden a plot and plan, divide it into quadrants, and plan a different selection of vegetables, herbs, and flowers for each. Make a "flagstone" path using white craft paper and a black, felt-tipped marker. Cut out the "stones" but save them to use during exposure.

Take the seed packets to a copy shop to have negative transparencies made. You can group five seed packets in a single shot, and then cut the images apart. Use a standard copy machine to copy the images onto repositionable transparency film; you may wish to enlarge the images. Then gather interesting fresh vegetables and gardening tools for other design elements.

Dip the sheet in a 16-gallon container of blueprint solution, thoroughly saturate it, and wring out the excess. You can save this solution for later use. The flannel sheet will be heavy and awkward when wet and

tipped marker; scissors; 2"-long T-pins or quilters' pins.

Wash the sheet three times in hot water to shrink it and remove lint and sizing. Dry it and plan your garden. To give your blue-

will require two people to handle (see instructions for the Faux Quilt). Dry the sheet in a household dryer, moving and fluffing it every ten or fifteen minutes to ensure thorough drying.

Fold the treated and dried sheet into fourths along the quadrant boundaries and smooth out all wrinkles. Lay out the path along the boundaries and arrange the seed packet transparencies, vegetables, and tools within one of the garden plots. Pin everything in place with 2"-long T-pins or long quilt pins. Pin the paper path within the black areas so that the pins will not appear on the blueprint. Anchor the "flagstones" so they won't blow away. Move the arrangement into the sun and expose it for ten or fifteen minutes as indicated by your test piece, removing the "stones" from the path two minutes before the end of the exposure time to soften the color.

Allow at least an hour to pin, expose, unpin, refold, position, and pin the next quadrant. Be sure to expose each quadrant for the same amount of time. If sunny time runs out, you can put the partially printed sheet in a light-proof bag and finish printing another day. (You must, however, finish exposing a quadrant before storing.) Though it's a slow process, by the end of the day, the blanket will be printed, rinsed, and dried. This "Garden Variety Blanket" needs no sewing or further attention.

I still have the seeds from the packets. Maybe this spring. . .

SHIRT/JACKET

I made up a pattern for this jacket, but it closely resembles Butterick pattern number 3324, and the same principles apply to any pattern you may choose.

For this jacket you will need 2 yards of

54"-wide or 3 yards of 45"-wide pretreated fabric; pattern pieces; support board a little bigger than the piece of fabric; pearl-headed sewing pins; scissors; sewing machine.

Trim around the paper pattern pieces, press them, and lay them out on a table or floor. The next step is to plan a design to fit the pattern or shape of the finished garment. Arrange the pattern pieces in the way that they will be sewn together. This will allow you to play with your design elements and arrange them in a logical or illogical fashion—whatever pleases you! Unless you have a photographic memory, take notes or label the elements once you've decided on your design.

Think about how you will anchor your design elements to the fabric and base. This forethought is necessary to reduce the time

Layout diagram for the Shirt/Jacket. Place the design elements as you want them to appear on the garment pieces.

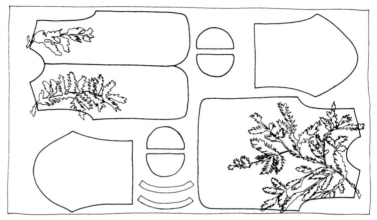

your treated fabric is exposed to light as you set up the design.

Next, take the pretreated fabric from its lightproof storage place and lay it out on the support board. Pin the fabric securely to the base. Position the paper pattern pieces on the fabric as they will be laid out for cutting. Remove one pattern piece and place the design element(s) for that piece on the appropriate section of the fabric. Secure the design element(s) with pins. Continue in

this fashion until all elements are secured, and then move the entire works into the sunlight for exposure. After desired exposure time, bring the fabric inside, remove the design elements and pins, and rinse thoroughly. When the print is fixed and the fabric dried, position the paper pattern pieces over the appropriate areas and cut them out. Follow the pattern instructions for assembly.

You may find that printing the entire

piece of fabric is too cumbersome—the support base has to be quite large and you may not have help in moving it outside. If this is the case, you can print the fabric in two steps. After removing the pretreated fabric from its lightproof storage place, fold it in half lengthwise with the right side out—if there is a right and wrong side. (This is how most commercial patterns are laid out.) You can now position the design elements for one half of the front, one of the sleeves, and one half of the back. The half of the fabric which is folded underneath and touching the support base will remain out of the light and will not print. After the first half of the fabric has been exposed, bring it inside, remove the design elements, flip the fabric over, lay out the elements for the second half, secure, and expose.

Another alternative would be to cut the pattern pieces out of the fabric before exposure. Use pinking shears to minimize ravels and cut the pieces slightly larger than they need to be—finish detailed cutting after printing. Pin the pieces to a support, secure the design elements, and expose them in managable groups, all for the same amount of time. If this is the method you choose, keep in mind that pretreated fabric will begin to react to indoor ambient light after being exposed for half an hour or so. Therefore work quickly and keep the light as low as possible. Finish the fabric as directed above.

WALL HANGING

This wall hanging is a simple project that will add an elegant decorator's touch to any room. The finished dimensions are 16" × 49".

For this project you'll need pretreated cloth measuring 17" × 51"; design elements; support board; pearl-headed sewing and long T-pins; sewing machine; 24"-long rod or dowel.

For this hanging, I cut bamboo shoots that looked to be just the right size and that had lots of fresh leaves. Unfortunately, the San Francisco summer fog refused to move and it was two days before I could print. When I was ready to print the fabric, the leaves had all shriveled up. But as I had my mind made up on the design, I simply removed the shriveled leaves, picked fresh ones, and placed them so that it appeared as if they were growing out of the shoots. If I ever want to repeat the design, I need only pick a few fresh leaves.

Bamboo leaves curl up almost immediately when exposed to direct sun. The stems are delicate and must be pinned down to stay in contact with the fabric. Place pearl-headed pins at the stem and leaf intersections and also across the leaf itself.

Three-dimensional objects such as bamboo shoots can be a bit tricky to print compared to flat objects or film. Pin the bamboo poles onto the support base using long T-pins. Pin the leaves next to the poles following a natural growth pattern. Angle the pins in such a way that they will not cast a shadow on the fabric. Expose, rinse, and dry in the usual manner.

Once your print is dried and pressed, turn under and sew a 1/2" hem along both long sides and the bottom. Turn the top edge under $1^1/_2$" and stitch in place. This will make a casing that you can use to hang the piece. Topstitch along the top edge a scant 1/16" to 1/8". Slide a 24" length of bamboo, dowel, or other rod through the casing. You can hang the piece by the rod with tiny nails, or you can attach a 30" length of string to the rod at each end and hang the piece by the string.

FOLDING SCREEN

This exquisite decorating accent is amazingly easy to make. The dimensions of each panel of this three-panel screen are 1' × 4'. Sprays of Chinese elm were used for the design source. You can follow the methods outlined here to create a screen that's the dimensions of your choosing.

For this project you'll need two pieces of sturdy pretreated cotton fabric (I used cotton twill) measuring $41^1/_2$" × $48^3/_4$" each; three pieces of 1/2" masonite cut to 1' × 4' each; design element; support board; pins; sewing machine.

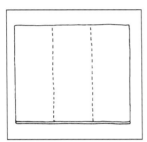

Make channels for the masonite by sewing two lines of stitching, top to bottom 13$^{1}/_{2}$" from each edge.

Plan your design, expose, rinse, and dry.

Make a 1/4" hem along the bottoms of each of the two blueprinted pieces of fabric. With right sides together, sew the two pieces together with a 1/2" seam allowance. Clip corners, turn right side out, and press. The piece should measure 40$^{1}/_{2}$" × 48". Add two lines of stitching 13$^{1}/_{2}$" from each edge, top to bottom, to form three channels. Slide one piece of masonite into each channel, smooth out any wrinkles, and set up the screen.

PRINTING WITH CHILDREN

Children are especially fascinated with the "magic" of blueprinting and they thrill at seeing familiar objects transferred to fabric. I've had resounding success working with children of all ages and abilities, and so can you with a little forethought.

Plan small, simple projects, especially when working with younger children, that are well within their capabilities. Preparing the support base, pinning the pretreated fabric to it, and securing design elements

in place require care and manual dexterity. Encourage children to use things they are familiar with as design elements and show them how to pin them to the support base.

Begin with projects that require little or no sewing or assembly. Preschool-aged children can print 12" × 18" pieces of cotton that can be used as placemats or sewn or bonded with Wonder Under onto simple pillows for nap time. School-aged children can print 8" or 10" squares to be mounted onto shirts, book covers, or aprons, assembled into a quilt, or made into flags. They can experiment with changing the color of a blueprint from blue to yellow to brown. As their confidence and capabilities improve, try bigger projects: clothing, charts of the galaxies, drama class backdrops, music class banners.

Pretreat the fabric yourself ahead of time or purchase pretreated fabric.

When blueprinting with children, keep

in mind the pace at which children work. It will take between 1 and $1^1/_2$ hours to get a group of children set up, get their designs pinned, moved outside to expose the prints, back indoors to rinse, lay out the prints to dry, and get everything cleaned up. Demonstrate the steps, suggest a time limit, set out the supplies, and get started. Pull the window shades and turn down the lights to minimize potential indoor exposure while they mount the pretreated fabric to support boards and set up their designs. While the room does not have to be dark, it should not be bright. If necessary, turn on an overhead light, but keep in mind that even artificial light sources contain some ultraviolet rays which will begin to change the color of pretreated fabric after about half an hour.

Plan in advance where the mounted designs will be placed outside and know what exposure time you want to use. Children want to know what to expect, where they are going, and what will happen next.

As with any activity that involves water, rinsing can quickly become a messy process when children are involved. Although most children love to play in water, you'll have to remind them frequently to rinse their prints vigorously and to continue rinsing until the water remains clear. I've found that the following bucket system works especially well with groups of five or more. Inside, out of direct sunlight, arrange layers of newspapers. On top of them, set a row of five or six 5-gallon buckets, each half filled with water. Have the children move from one bucket to the next, rinsing the fabric in each for a minute or so. When the water in the first bucket turns green, replace it with fresh water and then place that bucket at the end of the line so that it becomes the final clean rinse bucket. The simple ac-

tion of moving from bucket to bucket will encourage better rinsing, and thorough rinsing will ensure successful prints.

Be sure to have the children dry their prints inside away from direct sunlight. Like the rest of us, children will be anxious for the process to be complete. You can speed up the drying process using a hair dryer or by placing prints on a thick pad of newspaper and removing the upper sheets as they become wet. If you notice any blue color transferred from a print onto the newspaper below, quickly rinse the print again to prevent the image from disappearing by darkening and turning blue.

Most importantly, have fun! Encourage children to explore their natural curiosity and creativity. Don't be too quick to show them "the right way" to blueprint—let them come up with exciting new ways to print on their own.

Certificate of Chemical Safety

A chronic toxicity hazard assessment was done for blueprintable fabrics—fabrics treated with an aqueous solution of potassium ferricyanide and ferric ammonium citrate.

Potential exposure to the consumer can occur by dermal contact. Significant exposure by ingestion or inhalation is unlikely. The cyanide ion is tightly complexed with iron, and is released only under conditions of extreme heat or acidity. Therefore, exposure to toxicologically significant concentrations of hydrogen cyanide is unlikely.

Blueprintable fabrics were found not to pose a significant chronic toxicity hazard to the consumer. The criteria used for this evaluation are those published by the Consumer Product Safety Commission in the Federal Register, 16 CFR 1500, and current toxicological practice. Therefore, blueprintable fabrics meet the ASTM 4236 standard for chronic toxicity. No warning of chronic toxicity is required for this product.

—James. L. Byard, Toxicologist

Below is a copy of the care instructions that I provide with all of my blueprints, along with a sample swatch of blueprinted fabric. You may photocopy it and include it with all of your projects, too.

CARE INSTRUCTIONS

PLEASE READ THESE INSTRUCTIONS BEFORE WASHING!

• This is a photo image, not a dye. Although the print is permanent, the *blue will change to yellow if exposed to phosphates, soda, borax, chlorine, or peroxide.*

• Do not wash a blueprint in a machine in which powdered soap has been used; undisolved residues of powdered soap will discolor the blueprint.

• Recommended products: Only liquid, non-phosphate soaps such as Ivory, Joy, Dove, Palmolive, Tide, Wisk, or Woolite. (1/2 teaspoon per shirt.) Powdered, biodegradeable soaps are *not* recommended.

• A blueprint will not run or bleed. It can be line-dried inside or placed in a dryer. Iron if desired.

• Spot removers: I use Rit Grease & Stain Revomer #90. Use only *liquid, non-phosphate* spot removers. *Do not use undiluted soap for spot removal* (it will fade the blue color).

• Although handwashing is prefered, you can have a blueprint dry cleaned. Please have your dry cleaner test clean a swatch first.

• Avoid laundromats and commercial or public laundry facilities—the machines usually have traces of powdered detergent that will ruin blueprints.

BIBLIOGRAPY

Arnow, Janice. "Baby Face Quilt". *Sphere Magazine*, March 1974.

—. *Handbook of Alternative Photographic Processes*. New York: Van Nostrand Reinhold, 1982.

Schaff, Larry J. *Sun Gardens: Victorian Photograms by Anna Atkins*. New York: Hans P. Kraus, Jr., 1985.

FURTHER READING

Croner, Marjorie. *Fabric Photos*. Loveland, Colorado: Interweave Press, 1989.

Lowery, Jean Ray. *Imagery on Fabric*. Lafeyette, California: C & T Publishing, 1992.

Sims, Ami. *Creating Scrapbook Quilts*. Flint, Michigan: Mallary Press, 1993.

SOURCES

CHEMICALS:

Gramma's Graphics,Inc.
20 Birling Gap
Fairport, NY 14450
Send $1 plus SASE for brochure
Supplies chemicals in the porportion needed to treat approximately two yards of fabric.

Bryant Laboratory Inc.
1101 Fifth Street
Berkeley, CA 94710
(510) 526-3141
Supplies chemicals in one-pound units manageable for artists and craft projects. Will also sell 100-pound lots.

Spectrum Chemical Mfg. Corp.
14422 South San Pedro Street
Gardena, CA 90248
(800) 772-8786
Sells quantities up to 100 pounds.

READY-TO-BLUEPRINT FABRICS:

Blueprints-Printables
1504 #7 Industrial Way
Belmont, CA 94002
or
P.O. Box 1201
Burlingame, CA 94011
(800) 356-0445
Free brochure
Supplies pretreated fabric, T-shirts, sweat shirts, aprons, place mats, table runners, wall hangings, and kits packaged in lightproof bags. Nature Print® paper products, Nature Print® critter transparencies.Will treat natural fabrics or cotton sheets or blankets for printing.

GRAPHICS

Guard Litho
1206 South Amphlett, #3
San Mateo, CA 94402
(415) 341-8186
Will convert photographs to half-tone negative stats for use with blueprint-treated fabrics.

apron 34
Atkins, Anna *Children* 14, 15
banner 9
brown-tone prints 65
chemical solution, applying 23–25; disposal 28; formula for 22; lint 28; mold 28; preparing 21; storage 27
chemicals 12, 17
Children, John George 14
children, printing with 91–93
Chile Pepper T-Shirt 72
Circle T-Shirt 75
cleaning, dry cleaning 69; washing 68
color, problems 60, 61, 70, 71; removing 64, 65; restoring 67; sharpen contrast 61; variations 64–65
colored fabrics 62
cyanotype 12, 14
Daguerre, Louis Jacques Mande 12
daguerreotype 12
design set-up, nature prints 43–44; film 44–47;
design sources, fabrics 31; film, drawings, and text 35, 39; found objects 33; nature prints 29
diazo 16
drying 26, 61
exposure, temperature 49; timing 53
fabric, choosing 18; colored 62; hand-dyed 63; pretreating 19–20
fading 19, 70
Faux Quilt 81
ferric ammonium citrate 12, 17, 18
ferroferricyanide 17
film 35; continuous line 37; Kodalith 37; negative 36; positive 38; repeat use 47; repositional 47
Folding Screen 90
Garden Variety Blanket 83
glossary 40
halftone negative 36, 37
Herschel, Sir John 12, 14
images, positive and negative 32, 35
ironing 70
light box 51
lighting 20, 48–53
lights, artificial 50; mercury arc lamps 52; sun lamps 52; tanning lights 53; ultraviolet 50
nature prints 29, 43; pruning 30
negative image 32, 35, 38
overexposure 50
ozalid 16
Photo Album or Book Cover 79
photogenic drawing 12
photographs, choosing 35
Pillow 77
positive image 32, 35, 36
potassium ferricyanide 12, 17, 18
pretreating, lighting 20
print-on-a-print 31
printing, dry fabric 57; film 57; natural fibers 18; repeat 47; synthetic fibers 18; T-shirts 73; wet fabric 54–56; with children 91–93
projects 7, 8, 9, 10, 19, 32, 34, 36, 39, 71, 72–91
Prussian Blue 17
quilt 9, 10
rinsing 58
ruana 8
school projects 10
sepia 65
set-up 43
shawl 36
Shirt/Jacket 85
solution 21
spot, removal 69
support base 41
"suspenders" 45
sweatshirt 19
T-shirts 7, 19, 39, 48, 71, 72, 75
table cloth 10
Talbot, William Henry Fox 12
tank dress 32
tannic acid 66, 67
temperature, exposure 49
tie-dyed effect 23, 60, 82
underexposure 50
Van Dyke brownprint 65
Wall Hanging 88
washing 68
window shade 8
yellow-and-white prints 64